Modernizing Mexican Management Style

Modernizing Mexican Management Style

With Insights for U.S. Companies Working in Mexico

Eva Kras

Editts... Publishing

Modernizing Mexican Management Style
With Insights for U.S. Companies Working in Mexico
by Eva Kras

First Edition

Published by:
Editts... Publishing
P.O. Box 208
Las Cruces, NM 88001
Fax 505-523-1953

Printed and bound in the U.S.A.

Library of Congress Catalog Card Number: 93-74978

ISBN 1-884512-49-6 24.95

Table of Contents

Acknowledgements

The contents of this book I owe to many people who have generously shared their knowledge and experience and have given a great deal of their time so that others may benefit.

I owe deep gratitude to the many Mexican business executives who supplied the information used in this book. Seven companies that contributed greatly and beyond expectation by sharing "success stories" reproduced in this book are: CORPORATION ARGOS, S.A. DE C.V.; GRUPO INDUSTRIAL BIMBO, S.A. DE C.V.; INDUSTRIAS COMMONWEALTH, S.A.; PIGMENTOS Y OXIDOS, S.A. DE C.V.; TRANSMISIONES Y EQUIPOS MECANICOS (TREMEC) S.A. DE C.V.; COMPANIA SIDERURGICA DE GUADALAJARA S.A. DE C.V.; and VACOR DE MEXICO, S.A. DE C.V.. Additionally, many business leaders in many different regions of Mexico, too numerous to list individually, helped me to gain a deeper understanding of what is happening in Mexico today. Without their help, this book could not have been written.

I am also grateful to the authorities of Instituto Tecnológico y de Estudios Superiors de Occidente (ITESO) for their assistance, support, and encouragement, especially Jose de la Cerda for his valuable critique and suggestions, as well as the foreword he so kindly wrote.

My sincere thanks also go out to Roger Chartier, who generously gave of his time and knowledge to allow me to benefit from his wide research experience in the area of organizational change.

Last but not least, I want to recognize my ever patient and understanding husband, who served as my best critic and helper throughout this project.

Finally, I wish to express my appreciation to my publisher, who has understandingly and patiently guided me through the difficult exercise of editing and refining the manuscript.

Foreword

I never cease to be surprised that the traditional Mexican management style which, as Eva Kras observes, still predominates, is so similar to that observed by that North American professor, John Fayerweather, who came to do research in Mexico more than 30 years ago (*The Executive Overseas*, 1959). How is it possible to go on with such an outmoded management style for so many years without it defeating itself, biting its own tail like the proverbial serpent? If then the profile of traditional management as found by Eva Kras persists and still predominates, it deserves the sharpest criticism.

It is inadmissible that Mexican organizations should go on being managed by executives and managers incapable of forming teams, fearful of delegating responsibility and authority to their people, jealous of the development and creativity of their subordinates, dependent on family ties and influential relations, ignorant of the imperatives of quality and efficiency, and unaware of the loyal and devoted service of the common Mexican worker. Managers are self satisfied with their mediocrity and protected by their small domain of power. If this is how we Mexicans are when we direct people and organizations, then criticism is welcome, no matter how sensitive our culture has made us to adverse opinions about our ego and actions. We must overcome this obscurantism of Mexican management for the good of the country and future generations.

Nevertheless, as Eva Kras is careful to point out, it is necessary to find something valuable with which to supplant the worn out old ways. This transition in management means abandoning vices and bad habits which have got attached to our work culture. But this change must not harm our cultural values, which can, on the contrary, contribute to the development of a more efficient management norm, both in the use of available resources and in the distribution of the benefits accruing from the production of goods and services. Do we have any alternative? Can we be conformist or self-indulgent without losing those few but precious resources we still have in our country for the good of its inhabitants? No, managers, directors, executives, leaders, this is no time for inefficiencies. Now we are in full competition. We must not forget that we have lost a lot of time we should have used on preparation and experiments. Now we have to learn in the midst of competition, like the child learns to swim when he is thrown into the water. I am not saying that in the past management has always been inefficient, but there has been a lot of tolerance. Now the Mexican manager must work with a minimum of tolerance. Increasingly, we have to insist on ever greater quality.

Eva Kras' book can help us to become conscious of our cultural blocks, while at the same time fine tuning our administrative talents to overcome the shortcomings of so many Mexican organizations. There is no other way—the modern world is increasingly composed of organizations, rather than isolated individuals. Therefore, in Mexico, we have to learn to work in teams in intelligently managed organizations. Which are the elements that make an administration intelligent? Mrs. Kras provides us with an abundance of these. She takes up the best researched models of administrative theory and puts them to the test in successful Mexican businesses. Kras first questions and then verifies before proposing a model. The principles of modern administration which are put forward in this work are thus the result of a disciplined and insightful analysis, and although in administration we cannot yet speak of unassailable and universal principles, these are very promising. Let us hope that the managers of Mexican organizations and businesses decide to make the change towards total quality and find in this work a faithful and friendly guide.

Jose de la Cerda Gastelum
Guadalajara, Jalisco, April 20, 1990
Original Foreword to *La Administración Mexicana en Transición*

About the Author

Eva Simonsen Kras is a highly respected management consultant, writer, and speaker. During the past ten years she has conducted seminars and workshops designed to help U.S. and other foreign-owned businesses to overcome crosscultural management problems in their Mexican operations. She has held executive seminars for Bendix Corporation, Confad Group (Monterrey, NL), Ford Motor Company, General Electric, Hewlett-Packard, Johnson & Johnson, Kendall Corporation, Libby-Owens-Ford, Motorola, Sanyo Corporation, TRW Corporation, UNISYS Corporation, Western Maquiladora Association, Westinghouse Electric, and Grupo Vitro (Monterrey, NL).

Kras also is a researcher and part-time professor in the Master's Program in Business Administration—International Management at the Instituto Tecnológico y de Estudios Superiores de Occidente, Guadalajara, Mexico. Previously she was Senior Executive Personnel Manager, Ontario Division, The Hudson's Bay Company, where she wrote the Division's manual on personnel administration and co-authored the sales systems manual. She later lived abroad in several countries where she was exposed to different cultures and, in particular, to different approaches to management. These experiences have proven extremely valuable for the management research she has completed in Mexico.

In 1988 Kras published *Management in Two Cultures* which examined cultural issues that arise between U.S. and Mexican managers. In 1991 she published *La Administración Mexicana en Transición in Mexico. Modernizing Mexican Management Style* is based on the 1991 publication in Spanish, and has been updated to provide insights for U.S. companies working in Mexico. With the passage of NAFTA, this book promises to be timely in providing insights to businessman planning to work in Mexico and to students studying Mexican management at the university level.

Beside writing, research, teaching, and consulting, Kras currently is a partner in Bio Solutions Systems of Mexico. She has lived in Mexico for 18 years and resides in Guadalajara.

Introduction

"The lessons taught, while geared toward Mexican managers, are ones that should be taken to heart by all managers anywhere in the world who are concerned about long-term sustainability and the importance that cultural values play in implementing a modern management approach."

Modernizing Mexican Management Style identifies precise changes essential to respond to rapidly changing conditions facing Mexican companies today and ascertains the most practical ways to implement them for Mexican, U.S., and other foreign companies. This identification and assessment reflects first-hand experience of Mexican companies already moving toward a modernized approach to management and U.S. companies attempting to organize modern operations in Mexico.

This book, published as *La Administración Mexicana en Transición* in Mexico and adapted here, has been a concrete and practical handbook helping Mexican companies take the initial step of analyzing their present management style—including executives' attitudes and outlooks, and existing organizational approaches. It outlines basic steps that a number of Mexican companies have used successfully in transition from traditional to modern management. It presents a fundamental model of modern Mexican management that, when applied, results in changes in outlook, attitudes, and techniques essential to modernizing management. It also identifies specific issues U.S. companies need to consider when introducing modern management techniques in their Mexican operations.

Modernizing Mexican Management Style should be read by anyone wanting to understand the modernization process of Mexican management at the threshold of implementation of the North American Free Trade Agreement (NAFTA). It will help the expatriate executive working in Mexico in companies, such as multinationals and maquiladoras, with Mexican managers not yet exposed to modern participative management. It will help the managers and Head Office personnel of U.S. companies needing to understand how the transition process and the fundamentals of modern Mexican management differ from the U.S.

In many ways *Modernizing Mexican Management Style* is an outgrowth of Eva Kras's *Management in Two Cultures* (Intercultural Press, 1988). Research, seminars, and meetings with business executives related to that book led the author to conclude:

- Foreign executives planning to work successfully in Mexico need to adapt their management style to the Mexican cultural environment; and
- Mexican managers planning to perform successfully in the changed business environment created by Mexico's entry into GATT need to change from traditional to modern participative management approaches.

Eva Kras realized that further research into transitions in management styles in Mexican companies was essential to establish: What has already been accomplished in modernizing Mexican companies? What types of companies had modernized? What ingredients of management do these companies have in common?

Her research uncovered a small number of companies that have successfully attempted to alter traditional patterns to function effectively at various stages of modernization. They range from those nascent adopters breaking down "mentality barriers" to mature adopters who could teach lessons to Chief Executive Officers in the most advanced industrialized nations. Fundamental changes in management approach have been achieved in small, medium, and large

Mexican companies in several industrial regions. From these achievements emerges a modern management model, rooted deeply in Mexican cultural values, helpful for other Mexican companies to adapt, and useful to expatriate executives and scholars to learn how modern management can work effectively in Mexico.

Modernizing Mexican Management Style is organized in eight chapters:

Chapter 1, Gobalization of Management, describes the profound changes and new responsibilities that companies are now beginning to experience as a result of globalization and how these affect the management of companies in Mexico. It also outlines the differences that U.S. (and other foreign) companies are finding in the way modernization of management is perceived in Mexico as a result of changing international conditions.

Chapter 2, An Overview of Management in Mexico, describes the contemporary Mexican business and industrial scene which serves as the backdrop for the need for changes in management styles. It addresses questions such as: Why are changes necessary? What major risks are involved? Where are major changes needed? What are the major obstacles to change? What is the evidence for successful transition?

Chapter 3, The Process of Change, discusses the concept of change and resistance to change. It relates Kurt Lewin's field force analysis and Paul Lawrence's resistance to change to the process of change in Mexico, followed by a description of how this process affects U.S. companies working in Mexico.

Chapter 4, Cultural Values and Traditions in Mexican Organizations, addresses deeply rooted Mexican cultural values related to society and management. It attempts to separate fundamental values (family, religion, interpersonal relations), which must be preserved, from customs and habits (time and punctuality, commitment, ethics, superior/-subordinate relationships), which need to be modified or adapted should Mexican business survive. This is followed by an assessment of the issues which U.S. companies need to deal with related to these values and traditions.

Chapter 5, Management Styles Compared, a key chapter, compares significant aspects of traditional management with a paradigm for modern Mexican management. While necessarily drawing a stereotypical picture, the author describes management characteristics in this chapter that reveal dominant ones in Mexico today. The author presents a management model for Mexico that managers can implement, that has already been implemented successfully in some companies, and now is considered the basis for a Mexican modern management model. Then she relates the model to the issues U.S. executives will have to deal with when trying to modernize Mexican based companies.

Chapter 6, The Transition Process—Initial Steps, provides guidelines to initiate the process of change, based on the consensus of Mexican executives: Self-Analysis, Establishment of Overall Objectives, Development of the Management Team, Establishment of a Company Philosophy, Strategic Planning for Specific Goals, Team Development, Control and Follow-through, and Evaluation of Results. This chapter also discusses sensitization and communication in the Mexican environment and the adjustments that U.S. executives need to make when working in Mexico.

Chapter 7, Advice to Executives in Transition, provides practical advice for Mexican and U.S. managers to deal with the pitfalls and problems facing them during and after transition. These were gleaned from the extensive interviews conducted by the author with Mexican and U.S. managers. This follows with advice to U.S. managers during the transition to working in Mexico.

Chapter 8, Mexican Success Stories, presents seven case histories written by Mexican company executives. They talk about what they have done, how they did it, and what problems they met and continue to meet. These expositions show the great potential that exists among companies in Mexico to bring about the transition from traditional to modern management to be successful in the global marketplace.

At the conclusion of the book, the author provides a useful **Exercise for Self Analysis** that managers in Mexico and elsewhere could use for company self-analysis and evaluation.

Modernization of Mexican Management Style demonstrates that the Mexican CEO with a sincere desire to modernize management can do so, and this book provides useful guidance. The lessons taught, while geared toward Mexican managers, are ones that should be taken to heart by all managers anywhere in the world who are concerned about long-term sustainability and the importance that cultural values play in implementing a modern management approach.

Chapter One

The Globalization of Management

"The days of companies going into a country with short-term profit motives have passed."

Internationalization of Business

U.S. and other highly industrialized countries face new challenges when trying to work in a different environment. Their view of globalization, a term used to describe multiple aspects of the internationalization of business, usually emphasizes the point of view of a highly developed country setting up companies in developing countries. Today, however, companies working internationally face rapidly developing new responsibilities on the world scene. Those working in Mexico must also recognize those unique sensitivities that may make or break business relations in that country.

Companies with international operations are now entering a new phase which is causing much soul searching because situations are appearing that have no obvious parallels in the past for designing guidelines for solutions. For the first time in modern history, companies are faced with what appears to be severe limitations and stresses on Earth's capacity to cope with the contaminants and wastes that are produced by modern industrial development. At the same time, most companies view increased industrialization in developing countries as the best answer to increased prosperity in both first and third worlds. This is becoming an extremely controversial issue because if increased industrialization is to be considered viable in the long term, companies will have to find ways of eliminating pollution and controlling all wastes produced by their companies. The processes involved to achieve this objective are mostly costly, and governments as well as society at large must decide how the additional costs can best be paid. Some key questions are:

- Should companies be permitted to pass on the additional costs to the customer? Or should they be required to absorb the costs as part of the cost of producing a product?
- Should new prevention philosophies and procedures be instituted to reduce or eliminate the problems of wastes or pollution before they arise?
- Should a new method of calculating real costs of production be devised, whereby the use of air, water, and other natural resources are calculated according to their use and replacement possibilities?

These questions lead to another issue that is creating deep global concern—the rapid depletion of many natural resources as a result of rapid industrialization. Some of the natural resources presently being used in industry are in fact non-renewable resources, and ways need to be found to replace them or face their disappearance in the not too distant future. This will significantly change the focus of international business development for the future.

Of imminent concern is how these combined issues will transform the quality of life of the world's present and future generations. This is rapidly becoming an international issue, with evidence of increasing chronic unemployment, migrating populations in search of work and survival, and growing poverty combined with growing populations among the poorest communities in the world.

The concept of quality of life is now being accepted to include both a qualitative and a quantitative dimension. The emotional and spiritual well being of an individual must be taken into account equally with the basic requirements for physical survival. As poverty continues to increase in developing countries, particularly in spite of efforts to industrialize, and as modern technology spreads, employment patterns and potentials are being altered worldwide. The complex problem of quality of life is creating much concern for companies operating internationally.

According to many researchers in this field, a new era is dawning with the most dramatic changes since the Industrial Revolution. These changes influence profoundly the role of business organizations globally. For the first time business is being recognized as the most important force in the development focus of any country. Consequently, business organizations for the first time in history are beginning to be required to take responsibility for the focus of their own business development in foreign countries and to ensure that their company activities and philosophy are ones that benefit the country and its people in the long term. The days of companies going into a country with short-term profit motives have passed.

This newly developing environment alters completely traditional business practices and philosophies when going international. The globe and the survival of its people are now viewed with limitations. Business is gradually accepting the need to live within these limitation if indeed their businesses are to survive in the long term. This new situation is requiring a rethinking and a redirecting of the focus of international business. A few companies with visionary leadership are already reacting and transforming—that is, changing their mentality completely and thus the vision for their companies. These companies are also ones enjoying success in its broadest sense, both in the host country and at home. However, most companies are still struggling with the belief that some adjustments on the old approaches are enough, while a few are determined that the old way is the most sound solution.

Following are three fundamental global changes which are now being slowly accepted as essential for long-term business success in the international arena:

Human Priority over Economic Priority. This is a radical notion. The companies that have adopted this philosophy have transformed their management into a complete participative style. The basis for the success of this style is the introduction of team work at all levels of the organization. The companies that have adopted this philosophy are convinced of its advantages since they are enjoying both economic and human satisfaction benefits.

Community Integration. Decentralization of companies appears to be the focus for future viability. A new way of viewing the role of a company in the community is emerging. Gone is the era when a business chooses a location on purely profit motives for the company and considers that providing jobs should make the community satisfied. Many other considerations are now essential for the long term viability of the company.

Because ecological and natural resource factors are interconnected, companies now assess carefully the impact their company will have on the community. They now consider how their company will fit into the community. The workplace must be one in which the local population feels that their values and culture are integrated positively into the philosophy of the company. The company must be prepared to participate in and support community activities.

Win/Win Environment. The transformed company believes in a Win/Win philosophy as part of its company policy. Cooperation replaces confrontation and traditional Win/Lose competitive philosophy. This appears idealistic, but the few companies that have adopted this philosophy are convinced of its correctness and are thriving in the marketplace.

Globalizing Participative Management

One of the requirements for the transformation of companies internationally is the change to a human based focus. This change has been implemented through the adoption of a participative style of management. The key issue in transforming these companies, both in Mexico and the U.S., has been the need for a complete mentality change on the part of the CEO and top management. This is an extremely difficult step because it means totally discarding the traditional philosophy of doing business. For international companies, it is further complicated because the way it is practiced is linked to the different cultural environments in which the company works.

In the case of U.S./Mexican business combinations, a few key differences are pertinent to business success. These must be clearly understood and adjustments made accordingly before a U.S. company can hope to successfully transfer the concept of modern participative management to their Mexican operations. These main differences are:

Cultural: This includes deep cultural values, the way a person thinks, acts and reacts within the workplace.

Educational Background: This includes educational philosophy and focus.

Work Experience: This includes the type of work environment and responsibilities.

Management Style: U.S. companies are moving away from an individualistic responsibility focus toward a participative management style. Mexican companies are moving away from a traditional autocratic hierarchal style toward a participative management style. These different starting points require important adaptations in this transition.

In the following chapters, these differences in management styles will be analyzed and expanded to develop a clear picture of the adjustments essential for both Mexican and U.S. managers in the transition to modern participative management in a global market place.

Chapter Two

Overview of Management in Mexico

"Mexican CEOs must learn to preserve true cultural values and modify or eliminate customs and habits that hinder the achievement of company goals."

To describe a realistic setting for the principal subject of this book—the transition to modern management style in Mexico— the present business situation in Mexico and the vital part that management must play in its transformation must be discussed using these frequently asked questions:[1]

1. Why is change necessary?
2. What are the major areas in which changes are needed?
3. What are the main risks involved in proposed changes?
4. What are the major obstacles to change?
5. What are the positive indicators of successful change?

Necessity of Change

Mexico's current economic and political changes are the most radical and rapid since the Mexican Revolution. Entering into the

[1] José de la Cerda and Francisco Nuñez discuss these management changes and the need for change in La administración en Desarrollo: Problemas y Avances en la Administración en México, Mexico: Ed. Xache-te-ITESO, 1990.

General Agreement of Trade and Tariffs (GATT) has compelled Mexico to open up to the international marketplace, requiring Mexican industry to compete on the domestic market against the flood of imported goods entering the country. At the same time, many publicly owned enterprises have privatized and products and services previously reserved for the public sector have been deregulated. The resulting changes provide both opportunities and risks. How quickly and how well Mexican businesses respond and adapt to this new business environment will determine the success or failure of individual companies and the Mexican economy as a whole.

Risks of Change

Change inherently involves risks. A major risk is the danger of the closure of Mexican companies that are not flexible or cannot change quickly due to capital constraints, that do not produce products or services that compete well with those of foreign companies, or that simply do not wish to change. Also at risk will be Mexican companies that superficially change their approach to business in the global marketplace. A common example of a superficial change is the introduction of a new system in a specific department, hoping that this may provide a "quick fix" for all kinds of problems. Consequently, the CEO mistakenly believes that he has modernized his business, but has not fundamentally changed traditional approaches and attitudes that permeate the organization and prevent the transition to modern management style.

Another serious risk, of great concern to thinking Mexicans, is the loss of deep rooted cultural values (the total pattern of human behavior, beliefs, social forms, and customs, here related to the way Mexicans conduct business). Being pressured into making rapid fundamental changes in management style can profoundly uproot deeply held cultural values that identify Mexicans and gives purpose to their lives.

Some companies are thoughtlessly embracing foreign systems, theories, and processes with the intent of rapidly changing to successful foreign ways of doing business. By doing so, they have misjudged the consequences of this change on cultural values and indeed their whole way of life and that of their children. They run the risk of losing fundamental values and principles that guide their lifestyle, substituting for them values that may only be embraced superficially: values based on a consumerism based world view that is alien to their cultural heritage. This risk is real and is one area that management must guard against if they plan to evolve a new model that is harmonious with deeply rooted cultural values and is valid and applicable long term. Sacrificing cultural values for "modernism" would sacrifice that which almost every Mexican feels makes life worth living.

Areas of Change

The Mexican business community needs to address changes primarily related to attitudes toward competition and style of management:

Attitudes Towards Competition

Mexican business for many years has been protected from competition. Businessmen felt secure because high tariff barriers and government regulations isolated them from foreign competition. They worried little about markets. Small businesses had captive local markets, and larger companies marketed products nationally. Customers accepted what they got, seldom complained, and were generally loyal to their suppliers. Because of family ties or friendship between seller and buyer, if some prices were a little higher than the competitor's, the client mostly remained loyal. The seller sold almost anything and operated with a large profit margin based on low volume and a short-term time frame. This was a classical seller's market.

On the other hand, investment capital was limited, borrowing expensive, and economic conditions uncertain. The average businessman felt that basing himself on short-term considerations was the only viable course of action. Thus many Mexican products had a reputation for poor quality and service was often inferior. Nevertheless, a few companies always succeeded in exporting significant shares of their production. Sometimes cheap raw materials and labor favored them, but good modern management practices were necessary also to compete internationally.

Now the protected market has suddenly ended. As one Mexican CEO summarized it: "With Mexico's entry into GATT, we (Mexicans) have come to realize that we are living behind the times, especially as regards our inexperience in being competitive." No longer can business rely on protective tariffs and restrictions on goods entering Mexico; nor sell poor quality products; nor expect high profit margins; nor take the consumer for granted. Foreign competitors often can outprice them or offer goods of consistently better quality.

Mexico is rapidly moving from a seller's to a buyer's market. Now companies must stress quality products at competitive prices, excellent customer service, and prompt delivery—all while trying to overcome the inferior reputation Mexican products acquired. Dissatisfied Mexican customers may not complain, but they do quietly switch to other suppliers. Companies are forced into thinking long range, accepting reduced profits, but compensating with increased volume of business. All this comes as a shock to the Mexican business community, especially with the rapidity at which it has occurred.

Fortunately for Mexico, a few business people with foresight are planning and making changes necessary to meet this challenge. They serve as the examples for others to follow.

Style of Management

Mexican businesses divide into three main categories: 1) government owned and operated; 2) privately owned, and 3) multinational and foreign owned.

This book deals basically with privately owned Mexican companies, a group comprising large (2.1% and fairly modern in structure), medium (2.9%), and small (17.9% small and 77% micro, mostly traditional in management) businesses. The medium and small ones are most numerous, employ the majority of the work force, and contribute extensively to the economic and social stability of the country. They also need modernization the most, yet find it difficult to achieve.

Almost 100 percent of these companies are family owned and operated and have been managed traditionally for generations. The owner finds it difficult to release tight control over everything that happens and rarely feels the need, or has the ability, to train and develop a competent management team.

If these medium to small businesses want to survive, the present day owner-CEO must fully develop the potential of managers and staff. Owners cannot do it alone. They need to adjust their perceived role as CEO to concentrate on developing managers, delegating responsibility and authority, and increasing participation of all employees. To become role models for subordinate managers, CEOs need vision, knowledge, and empathy. In the process they will establish a management team in which all are integral members, including the CEO, and each feels free to contribute meaningfully. The problem this new paradigm presents, as summarized by one CEO who already has completed this change, is that "The CEO's greatest obstacle is himself."

Obstacles to Change

The two main obstacles to change are distinguishing between deep cultural values and bad habits and adapting to participative management: 1) traditional image style, 2) education, and 3) theory vs practice.

Deep Cultural Values vs. Bad Habits and Customs

As in most countries, much resistance to change in management in Mexico resides in the context of cultural background. Within any Mexican organization, certain values and assumptions predominate. These translate into recognizable mental traits, attitudes, and customs that profoundly influence the way business is done. Some of these are important cultural values that must be preserved. Others are customs and habits that have developed and become ingrained through the years, and many of these have proved a discouragement to productivity, efficiency, and job satisfaction.

Mexican CEOs must learn to preserve true cultural values on the one hand and on the other modify or eliminate customs and habits that hinder the achievement of company goals. The initiation of this change falls squarely on the shoulders of the CEO. In most cases this requires a complete mental overhaul—a fundamental change in the CEO's traditional assumptions and habits. As one CEO said: "We have to accept that certain customs and habits will have to go." Companies having already made the break agree that this is the most difficult step. Without the CEO's complete conviction and commitment, however, nothing worth while or long lasting will be achieved.

Change to Participative Management Style

The transition to real participative management faces many obstacles, chiefly: 1) the traditional image of the owner or CEO, 2) the educational background of employees entering the company, and 3) the emphasis on theoretical rather than practical thinking.

Traditional Image

The role CEOs play in companies must undergo a complete transformation. First, they have to train and develop managers to handle completely delegated responsibility and authority. Total control cannot be retained exclusively by the CEOs, nor can they expect managers to do only what they are told.

To set a good example for participative management, CEOs must demonstrate the ability to work with and within the management team, thus effecting a reversal of the traditional concept of hierarchy and authority. As an experienced modern CEO said: "The biggest change in Mexico is in the role of the leader. His concept of status must change from appearing (creating an image) to being." These changes will be discussed in detail later in this book.

Education Backgrounds

Many executives of progressive Mexican companies acutely recognize the obstacle to modernization inherent in the educational background that graduates bring into the firm. Most CEOs interviewed believe that the majority of Mexican graduates are severely deficient when entering the organization. First, they lack depth in their chosen field of specialization due to pressure to cover many subjects and amass a lot of facts, often treated insufficiently to make knowledge directly applicable on the job. Second, their education emphasizes theory without a bridge to practical application, making the transition from classroom to job extremely difficult. Furthermore, most graduates have not developed inquiring minds because of limited emphasis on analytical thinking and practical problem solving in their educational programs. The young executive finds it difficult to apply knowledge in day-to-day work which requires problem analysis and concrete decision making.

Many federal and state authorities recognize these problems and are attempting to modernize Mexican public education. The main obstacle to change, according to Juan Prawda, is the built-in inertia of the system: "The greatest difficulty will undoubtedly be the bureaucratic inertia and the resistance of some education authorities, by some of the teachers' unions and by some of the teacher training colleges that supply secondary schools with new teachers, which might view this model as an invasion of their exclusive territory."[2] As a result, change is too slow to keep pace with modernization taking place

[2] Juan Prawda, "Teoría y Praxis de la Planeación Educativa en México, México, Ed. Grijalbo, S.A., 1985, p. 261.

in the business world. Only a handful of schools and universities provide the quality education called for, and from these schools are drawn many of Mexico's business leaders.

The new competitive forces impinging upon Mexican business obliges the most advanced firms to keep abreast of technological developments in the industrial countries. They are experiencing a severe shortage of Mexican graduates with up-to-date knowledge to apply these technologies.

While this problem is not unique to Mexico, it considerably slows the pace of modernization. University leaders, while conscious of the problem, realize that they do not have the resources to overcome this problem without substantial aid from industry.

Industrial leaders recently have given more support to higher education, with the prospect that industrial-education cooperation will grow and have the desired results. Presently, however, the companies undertake most of the training of employees in situ or by sending them to specialized courses conducted by equipment suppliers at home or by organizations abroad.

In the field of management education, a few leading educational institutions have established solid reputations for the high professional performance of their graduates. These are examples of what can be achieved by Mexican education institutions, and their graduates are sought after.

Theoretical vs. Practical

Modern managers consider that the transition from theoretical thinking to practical action poses one of the most difficult problems to overcome during the transition process. While the root of this problem lies mainly in the focus of the educational system, other aspects of Mexican culture and tradition play a part. One is the general disdain Mexican society has had for manual work. This attitude favors intellectual and artistic activities at the expense of practical ones. Intellectual work is perceived as having certain cultural value and prestige. The emphasis on the development of theoretical and conceptual abilities at school and university further encourages the graduate to use these well developed abilities rather than the less developed practical skills. This reflects the frequently observed phenomena of the gap between words (good intentions) and deeds (doing the job) and between starting a job and finishing it. It hampers detailed planning, control, and follow-up.

The frequent subjective attitude toward practical work is incompatible with modern business needs and will have to be modified for Mexico to compete successfully in the new global marketplace.

Positive Indicators of Change

Most Mexican managers and workers possess many attributes that can be turned to great advantage, as demonstrated in the examples to be cited later in this book. Their full potential has barely been tapped.

Factors that contribute most to successful management transformations are:

- intelligence
- creativity
- flexibility
- resourcefulness.

When these are cultivated by a CEO who challenges employees and demonstrates confidence in managers' ability to make fundamentally required changes, Mexican business has overcome obstacles to change and progressed toward modern management style.

Chapter Three

The Process of Change

"Most U.S. companies setting up operations in Mexico try first to introduce individual thinking and accountability in managers and then continue from there to introduce participative management concepts from a U.S. viewpoint. As a result most U.S. companies have experienced extensive frustration and few have identified the root of their management difficulties."

Change Research

The process of change has been researched extensively in the most highly industrialized countries. This research has accompanied the changing economic conditions that have been part of the world business scene for generations. The great amount of literature published, mainly in the U.S., analyzes the basic characteristics of change and the various ways of handling resistance to change.

According to Kurt Lewin,[1] the process of change occurs in three clearly defined steps or levels:

Unfreezing: In this process of dissolving present habits, behaviors or routines, the recipient is made to feel the disad-

[1] Kurt Lewin, *Field Theory of Social Science*, New York: Harper and Row, 1951

vantages and lack of value of the present situation and the positive potential for changing particular behavior or routine.

Change: Once motivated and ready to discard the old ways, the individual receives new models of conduct (or processes) that replace the old. Everyone adopts the new model and tries hard to follow its criteria in daily working life.

Refreezing: In this process, the new habits, behaviors and work processes become part of everyday life and are established as a permanent replacement for the old.

Forces for Change

Field Force Analysis

Kurt Lewin sees two main opposing forces at work in the change process. One is a field force that encourages change, and the other is a restrictive force that resists change. In every organization both exist and are in a state of relative equilibrium while the organization operates at consistently high levels of productivity and quality. However, when change becomes necessary, one force must gain the advantage over the other. Lewin has represented this process graphically in Figure 3.1

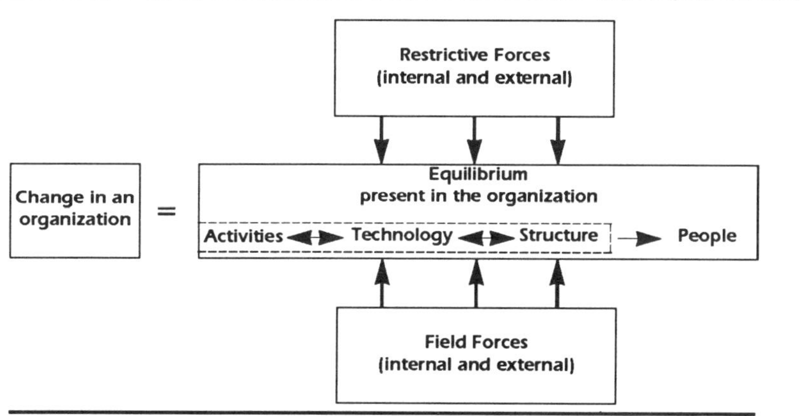

Figure 3.1: The Process of Organizational Change (cf. K. Lewin)

As noted, these two opposing forces are also subject to internal and external influences—influences from within and outside the organization. How these forces manifest themselves in a business organization is seen below.

Restrictive Forces: These forces oppose the field forces through apathy, passivity, hostility, and generally through poor work performance.

External Forces: These may include tradition, customs, social and family pressures, lack of vision of social and community groups in accepting the need for change, and resistance of support services to change.

Internal Forces: These are traditional role models and interpersonal relationships, sense of security in present position versus the unknown, lack of perception of the necessity or urgency for change, lack of confidence in the leader's intentions, and a natural inertia tending to maintain the status quo.

Field Forces: These forces are directed and propelled by such factors as competition in productivity and quality, pressure from the superior, the use of incentive programs and, sometimes, the CEO pushing for modernization.

External Forces: These include, in the case of Mexico, the entry into GATT and its accompanying competition, the struggle to stay in business and maintain jobs, and the need to improve quality and productivity.

Internal Forces: In Mexico these include pressure by top management for productivity, quality, involvement of managers in planning and decision making, new structures and the increased participation sought by employees at all levels, and greater emphasis on the human side of work and the working environment.

From this point, Lewin proceeds to develop the different levels and cycles of change that occur within an organization. This is demonstrated graphically in Figure 3.2 (following page). When the change begins with the individual and progresses upward through the company, one begins at the bottom of the chart and moves upwards through the different steps. On the other hand, the process can also be inverted, when the change is instituted from the top of the organization and penetrates down the different levels to the individual.

According to Lewin's chart below one distinguishes two different cycles of change: 1) the Individual Participation Cycle and 2) the (Senior Management) Imposed Cycle.

In the Participation Cycle the power of the individual begins at A and rises to point B—it begins with new knowledge, then changes in individual attitudes, follows with conduct, and finally spreads to the behavior of the whole group. This kind of cycle usually occurs

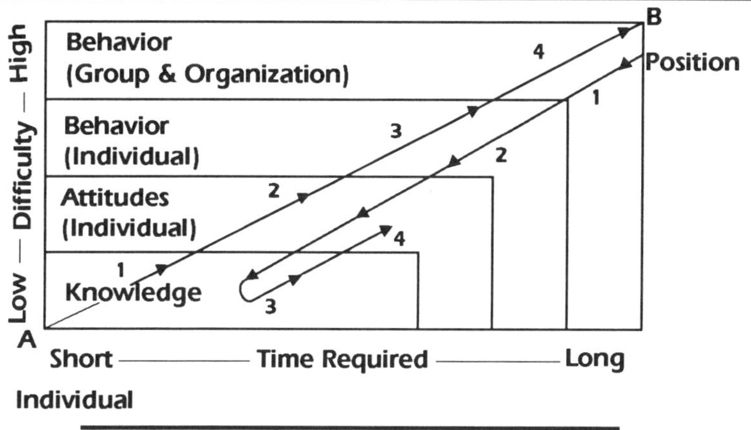

Knowledge: easy and rapid change; information, written or oral, advice.

Attitude: most difficult change; emotions are involved.

Individual Behavior: change is slow and difficult; involves habits and social controls; example—smoker.

Group and Organizational Behavior: change is very slow and difficult; collective reinforcements and interaction, traditions, customs.

Figure 3.2: Levels of Change: Difficulty (effort) & Time Required (cf. K. Lewin)

in mature groups that are achievement oriented, knowledgeable and experienced, very responsible, and work under an open and flexible leadership. This cycle of change usually begins slowly, evolves over a considerable time, and produces lasting change.

In the Imposed Cycle the power of top management at point B imposes change on a broad scale covering the whole organization, which gradually works its way down to each group (level) and finally reaches the level of the individual (point A) and his behavior. However, on the last two steps the new knowledge is preceded by the development of new attitudes. This imposed cycle is usually found in less mature groups that are dependent, lacking in sense of responsibility, fearful, and externally motivated. The process is more rapid, but less secure and lasting.

Resistance to Change

In spite of the time elapsed since his study was published,[2] Paul Lawrence is probably one of the most respected authorities on the phenomenon of resistance to change. He says that "people don't resist technological change in itself, and the major part of the resistance which occurs is usually unnecessary." Going from there, he outlines some of the key considerations in the process:

1) The people affected must participate in the change. People react to the way they are treated. If they are allowed to participate in the change, people feel valued and respected as individuals.
2) The key is to understand the nature of the resistance. It is usually to be found in the social aspect of the change.
3) Resistance at the lower level usually arises as a result of blind spots and specific attitudes displayed by the management.
4) Emphasis must be placed on norms of behavior and attitudes for all management.

[2]Paul Lawrence, "How to Deal with Resistance to Change," *Harvard Business Review*, 1954, v. 32, n. 3, pp 49 and 56.

5) Upper management can be more effective in their meetings with subordinates if they, in place of concentrating their attention exclusively on the execution of a project, technical details, and assignment of tasks, concentrate on observing what the discussion of these matters indicates with regard to the development of resistance or receptivity to change.

Lawrence warns: "When resistance appears, one should not consider it as something to be conquered. Instead, it is better to consider it as a useful 'red light'—a signal that something is going wrong. One must go back and redefine the job to be done and identify what went wrong."

Lawrence goes on to define the role of the administrator (CEO) in the process as:

- treating managers as they should treat their subordinates,
- coordinating different groups of people involved in change, with primary responsibility for facilitating communication and understanding of different points of view, and
- discussing time management, technical details, and assignments while being alert to the 'messages' sent out in group discussions and asking key questions related to how comments are perceived, what can be said, what is understood, and what does one support or oppose.

Lawrence further asserts that when CEOs show concern for problems and act to promote understanding, common purpose is served better and new ideas and technological change are put into practice. In summary, "The resistance to change is an important signal which demands that management becomes better informed about what is really going on."[3]

[3] Ibid. p 56.

The Process of Change in Mexico

Mexican management transition is traumatic because of the need to change culturally conditioned behaviors, attitudes, and outlooks and to embrace new management practices and techniques.

Lewin's theory assumes that the change process takes place in an established society—one not undergoing any far-reaching cultural changes. In Mexico required changes are radical, involving both culture and management style; they affect both the world of work and the entire outlook on life.

Some Mexican companies have tried to introduce some aspects of modern management by superimposing them on traditional cultural behaviors. The results consistently have been disappointing from both the standpoint of productivity, quality, and human resource development. This is illustrated in Figure 3.3.

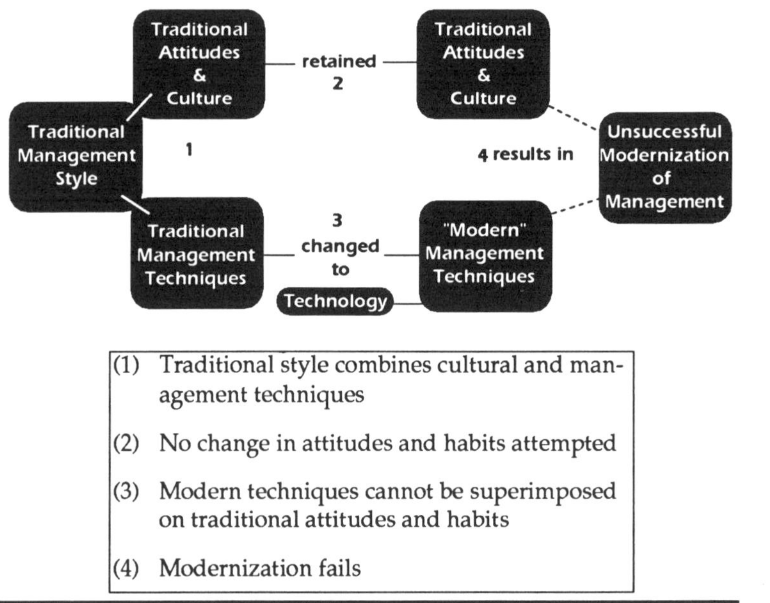

Figure 3.3: Superimposed Modern Management Resulting in Failure to Change

First, (1) traditional management style combines both cultural and management techniques. Second, (2) changes in attitudes and culture are retained. Third, (3) modern management techniques are attempted to be superimposed on traditional attitudes and habits. Fourth, (4) modernization fails.

On the other hand, a few Mexican companies have made fundamental cultural changes alongside changes in management style. These companies have been remarkably successful and are widely accepted as models for modern Mexican management. This is illustrated in Figure 3.4.

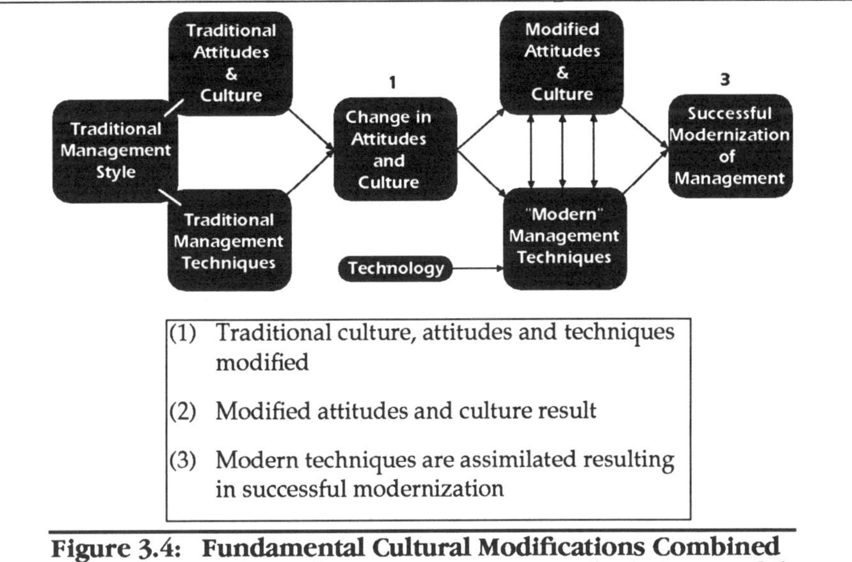

Figure 3.4: Fundamental Cultural Modifications Combined with Modern Management Results in Successful Change

First, (1) traditional culture and attitudes and techniques are modified. Second, (2) modified attitudes and culture result. Third, (3) modern techniques are assimilated resulting in successful modernization.

Experience clearly shows that in Mexico new management techniques cannot be imposed successfully on traditional cultural patterns. This additional step is required: a change must first take place in traditional customs and habits. These are modified and replaced with new ones oriented toward total development of the human resource potential. As discussed in Chapter 3, these affect not the deeply held cultural values that must be preserved, but instead the whole gamut of traditional customs and habits that stand in the way of the successful implementation of a modern management style. The process of cultural change in Mexico, described later in this book, has been accomplished in many different ways.

Insights for U.S. Companies in Mexico

The changes required for U.S. managers working in Mexico are in some ways more complex than for Mexican managers making the transition to modern management, even though the basic process is similar. U.S. management will need to bear in mind the following:

Cultural Adaptation: U.S. management needs to adapt to Mexican culture and learn to differentiate those deeply ingrained cultural values in Mexican management that must be preserved from those developed habits and customs that need to be modified.

Management Style: U.S. management style stresses individualism and personal accountability while the traditional autocratic Mexican style requires managers to respond to specific instructions and maintains decisions making and control in the hands of the CEO.

Transitional Process: U.S. companies are moving to a participative management from a different base than Mexican companies so that deep changes in approach will need to be developed when working in Mexico.

Most U.S. companies setting up operations in Mexico try first to introduce individual thinking and accountability and then continue from there to introduce participative management concepts from a U.S. viewpoint. As a result most U.S. companies have experienced much frustration and few have identified the root of their difficulties. The following analysis of how the Mexican process has developed, when related to the U.S., will help U.S. managers better grasp the basis for inherent differences and thus more successfully cross the hurdles of the transition.

Chapter Four

Cultural Values and Traditions in Mexican Organizations

"...upon first meeting a Mexican counterpart, the U.S. manager often concentrates on the Mexican manager's capabilities and knowledge, while the Mexican manager concentrates on the U.S. manager's personal qualities."

Challenges Facing U.S. Companies

One of the most complex challenges facing U.S. companies trying to do business in Mexico is adapting to Mexican organizations' cultural values and traditions. As described in *Management in Two Cultures,* the family maintains the central value in life, and work must adapt to those requirements. Hand in hand with the family is religion which forms the basis for most Mexicans' perception of self, relationship with others, spirituality, and world view. Many perceptions that a U.S. manager would consider normal are different in Mexico. This creates gaps in understanding of basic human relationships in the workplace.

When entering Mexico for the first time, the U.S. manager must realize that he will start off on the wrong foot should he prioritize tasks over human elements. For example, upon first meeting a Mexican counterpart, the U.S. manager often concentrates on the Mexican manager's capabilities and knowledge, while the Mexican manager concentrates on the U.S. manager's personal qualities. The U.S. manager thinks: "Can this person do the job adequately?" The Mexican thinks: What type of person is he? Can I trust him? Can we work together well? Does he have some values similar to mine? How does he feel about Mexico? The U.S. manager focuses on the needs of the task ahead and feels that these other aspects are ones that will take care of themselves as work progresses.

These immediate perceptual gaps upon first meeting increase over time, especially with regard to the concept of sensitivity. Problems with sensitivity are proportionally related to the degree to which the U.S. manager has been able to gain the trust and confidence of the Mexican manager. If the U.S. manager has stressed human concerns from the outset, sensitivity problems diminish and the Mexican manager begins to feel trust and confidence in his U.S. counterpart. He begins to be more open and his motivation to work is heightened to optimal potential.

The U.S. manager also has difficulty understanding work environment in Mexico. Mexicans seldom thrive in a stressful work environment or one that encourages competition among colleagues. The Mexican prefers an harmonious human centered environment. U.S. managers often find this difficult to understand because they thrive on the stimulation of a competitive environment and its accompanying stress.

Customs and Habits to be Changed

To help facilitate the modification of negative habits and customs, the U.S. manager will need to move carefully. He will need to get the full confidence and commitment of his Mexican counterparts and they will be the ones to introduce the necessary changes with the Mexican work force. Without this agreement, the Mexican manager and the workers will tend to feel it an imposition of American ways in Mexico. Many of these habits which require modification are already recognized by Mexican managers. The challenge to the U.S. manager is to gain the confidence of the Mexican manager, take his advice as to how the changes can be approached, and then support him every step of the way.

Cultural values[1] and traditions influence almost everything a Mexican does daily: the way work is done, interpersonal relationships, perceptions of the wider world, spirituality, and his perception of himself as an individual. These involve deeply held beliefs, values and assumptions that reflect the essence of the value of his life and establish his identify as a Mexican.

Other customs have evolved through the years as habits and behaviors that are comfortable and provide a framework for knowing what to expect in any given situation, be it at work, at home, or in the community.

This book divides cultural phenomena into two groups:

- those deeply ingrained cultural values that are fundamental to the social and moral stability of the country and must be preserved; and
- those customs, habits, and behavioral traits that are not ingrained cultural values and may be detrimental to modernization. These latter have been shown to be amenable to modification and adaptation during the transition to modern management style in Mexico.

Ingrained Cultural Values

Family

Mexicans value family above all else. The family is the glue that holds society together, and from it stems bonds of trust, responsibility, strong affiliation, and emotional support that gives meaning and purpose to life. In general, children grow up loved, protected, and at-

[1] Cultural values as used here is taken to mean the totality of behavioral patterns, social forms, and beliefs, particularly those that affect the way business is done in Mexico.

tached emotionally and closely to the family. This strong familial affiliation carries over into the workplace where strong hiring preference is given to family members and close friends of the family of the owners and trusted employees. These familial relationships help to create a comfortable atmosphere of trust, confidence, harmony, and solidarity in the workplace. As a result, the workplaces tends to be viewed as an extension of the home—the owner or CEO replaces the father as the authority figure, and subordinates obey orders and do as they are told.

This system still flourishes in small family businesses. But as businesses grow and more highly differentiated skills are needed, this authoritarian family structure requires significant modification. These modifications do not diminish the importance of close family ties at all levels of society. Loyalty to family remains central in the individual's life. As one senior executive said: "If we touch the family, we touch the very roots of Mexican society."

Religion

The Roman Catholic Church strongly influences Mexico's basic cultural values. Christian values taught by the Church permeate the fabric of society, even though not all Mexicans are regular churchgoers. The Roman Catholic Church is seen as providing cohesion in Mexican society. It provides fundamental moral values, affirms the individual's self esteem and respect for others, and influences Mexicans' relationship with nature and the spiritual world. This results in a quite consistent emphasis on respect for the dignity of the individual and courtesy, which in its broadest sense forms part of upbringing or education.

In a country with widespread poverty, religion provides solace, peace of mind, acceptance of fate, and courage to struggle on in spite of suffering and apparently insurmountable odds. Religion overall has contributed much to maintain social peace during Mexico's painful upheavals. Despite all the stresses in Mexican society, the

Church remains a strong force in preserving the deep cultural values of Mexico.

A number of executives interviewed believe that the role of the Roman Catholic Church is shifting as a result of the modernization process toward placing greater emphasis on personal effort and individual responsibility for one's actions.

Interpersonal Relationships

Mexicans attach great importance to interpersonal relationships. The human element is key in all transactions, at all levels of society, in both private and public sectors of the economy. Mexicans relate to people, not to products or services. This "Mexican way of doing things" contrasts sharply with the Anglo-Saxon business approach that emphasizes task before person. Personal respect and recognition motivate Mexicans. Personal relationships must be nurtured and cultivated carefully to gain commitment from the work force to maximize efficiency and productivity. The modern CEO, therefore, must be aware of the deeply rooted value placed on personal relationships. Once these are established, workers more readily identify with the company and its goals.

Interpersonal relationships that affect the running of a modern Mexican enterprise pertain to these five important aspects of human resource management: 1) Person versus Task, 2) Emotional Sensitivity, 3) Etiquette, 4) Work and Recreation, and 5) Work Environment.

Person versus Task

Industrialized countries tend to place priority on tasks to be performed and to view the person as a vehicle through which the job is performed. This view minimizes the importance of the person as an individual—he is primarily a tool for the efficient functioning of the organization. Mexicans believe this dehumanizes the workplace. When respect for the dignity of the individual is a central cultural value one expects first to consider whether the person—in terms of character, personality, and knowledge—would be happy performing the task. Establishing this should result in good performance because the person has been considered before the task. This means that it is important for the boss to know his subordinates well. Recognizing "personal" value is essential for successful management in Mexico.

Emotional Sensitivity

Emotional sensitivity of Mexicans should come as no surprise given the emphasis on interpersonal relationships. This sensitivity relates closely to the aesthetic nature of Mexicans, and both aspects are clearly evident in the workplace. Aesthetic manifestations range from flowery language to pomp and ceremony on festive occasions.[2] They also manifest themselves in creative ideas for solving problems and innovations in the work process. Inside or outside work the whole person reacts to a situation.

As an emotionally sensitive person, the Mexican is apt to take all work criticism personally. Mexicans have thus evolved a sophisticated art of diplomacy to deal with criticism, delegation of work, and correcting and checking work in progress. Without this diplomacy the Mexican would feel attacked personally. An executive criticized in front of colleagues or subordinates or treated without due dignity and respect would regard this as loss of face, loss of status, and could even resign.

Emotional sensitivity, however, diminishes when a person gains confidence in his boss and gains his support for decisions—right or wrong. A great deal hinges on the superior's ability to build up a relationship of trust and confidence with his subordinates.

Etiquette

Etiquette—the expression of the Mexican's courtesy and regard for others— is of utmost importance as a sign of education and good

[2] Juan F. Zorrilla treats this subject in "Jocosidad y estructura social en una fábrica de henequén,' in Viviana B. Márquez, (Ed.) Dinámica de una empresa mexicana: perspectivas económicas y sociales, Mexico, El Colegio de México, 1979.

breeding in Mexico. Persons who violate accepted norms lose the respect of their superiors, colleagues, and subordinates. Persons who observe accepted norms are respected and considered *educado*. Parents teach children good manners and behavior at an early age and expect them to observe norms when in contact with all age groups—and especially with adults and older people. Children learn to show respect and consideration for anyone older than themselves or in position of authority. Etiquette is adjusted to different social classes and particular social situations.

Modern business adheres to traditional notions of etiquette as essential to the smooth running of a modern company. In traditional businesses authoritarian executives sometimes abuse lower level employees. This offends their dignity and undervalues their work and effort. Employees so affected quickly lose commitment to their work and loyalty to their company.

Work and Recreation

Mexicans believe that work needs to be balanced with recreation (which mostly involves time spent with family and close friends). Happiness requires both work and recreation. An imbalance toward work threatens family life, and thus strikes at the heart of a central value. This imbalance leads to unhappiness and poor work performance and attitudes. The average Mexican worker or manager believes that work is important and is prepared to expend long hours when necessary, especially when he has good leadership. But balance is needed to avoid overload that harms family relationships.

Work Environment

Mexicans need an harmonious work environment. An environment of confrontation, competition (between individuals within the company), and stress creates an atmosphere that most Mexican find intolerable and incompatible with good job performance. For optimum performance and job satisfaction, Mexicans search for companies that have an amicable, atmosphere. (Many of the Mexican executives interviewed said they needed an harmonious atmosphere to perform at their best.) They usually try to leave companies with unsettling atmospheres as quickly as possible, regardless of how satisfactory their salary may be.

Customs and Habits that Need Modification or Change

Apart from the deep cultural values discussed above, a number of deeply ingrained traditional behavior patterns exist, generally classified as customs and habits. Only a few of these have a negative effect in business. Fortunately these are susceptible to change and already have been radically modified in companies that have made the transition. The most important ones, discussed below, are: 1) Time and Punctuality, 2) Concept of Commitment, 3) Ethics, 4) Relationship with Superior, and 5) Individual versus Team.

Time and Punctuality

The disregard for time in Mexico is most noticeable and highly frustrating for businesses. That time is vague and elastic still prevails in most parts of the country. More people recognize, however, that time consciousness is essential should Mexico succeed in modernizing its industry and commerce to compete internationally.

One consequence of using time imprecisely is the tendency to estimate time to completion of task overly optimistically. This is done to please the other person. At the time it is done, the only concern is being able to please—consequences of being unrealistic are not of concern. Clearly, behavior toward time needs major modification to establish the importance of long-term credibility over short-term pleasure.

The vagueness of the time concept in Mexico poses many other obstacle to modernization. Among these are:

- inability to organize one's time,
- lack of commitment to deadlines,

- inattention in appointments and time commitments (for example, keeping clients waiting or making them return another day),
- failure to keep appointments (and covering up with a feeble excuse), and
- having to redo a job badly done, and not feeling responsible for the client's wasted time.

In all these respects Mexico needs to improve its use of time.

Concept of Commitment

The traditional Mexican subordinate tends to optimistically estimate time to please his boss, regardless of the probable consequences of failing to fulfill them. It is still common to regard commitments as mere statements of good intentions instead of committing one's personal integrity. Since traditionally good intentions carry almost as much weight as the actual fulfillment of a commitment, they often substitute for action. Many Mexicans accept this situation with resignation in daily life, including business. The underlying motivations for doing this need significant modification, and gradually managers and workers are starting to assume personal accountability.

Ethics

Ethics develop during childhood at home, in church, and in school. The Mexican child is exposed to the strict moral code of the Roman Catholic Church. However, the attitude toward telling the truth in the strict sense is modified by the sensitive nature of the Mexican's attitude toward interpersonal interaction. Children learn that one does not say anything that will hurt the feelings of others. At a young age they hear parents tell 'little white lies' or half truths to protect sensitivities. As adults this trait becomes second nature. In the work place, they will 'modify' an answer or statement to avoid conflicts or confrontations with the boss or colleagues. This is not considered unethical, but it creates severe problems at work when commitments are unfulfilled or results do not meet expectations.

Related to this aspect of ethics is the acceptance of copying or cheating in school. It is acceptable for children to help others—which can include copying homework and exams to help a friend. It is common to use *acordeones,* crib notes that are used to "help remember" key points during an exam. As children become older, pressure increases to succeed at school and obtain their qualifications. Thus the practice of copying and other more serious manifestations still persist at educational institutions. While most school authorities try to stamp out these practices, they are deeply ingrained and difficult to eradicate—both among students and even some teachers.

By the time of graduation young people have been extensively exposed to many gray areas of ethics. Some rationalize this behavior as an acceptable part of culture and embrace this as "the best way to get things done and to be successful." Others reject this behavior as dishonest and vow not to do business this way. Fortunately, more business people are inclined toward this latter group. Changes in the political and economic climate are gradually reducing the scope for unethical practices and changing the balance between rewards and penalties. Most business people all over Mexico are anxious to modify the gray areas of ethics, but the process is slow, since tradition and interpersonal arrangements still exert significant influence.

Relationship with Superior

In the workplace the owner traditionally is the authority, omniscient and omnipotent. He acts like the father at home who imposes his wishes, makes all decisions, solves all problems, and hands out punishment. The employee, in return for receiving the opportunity to work, is expected to respect and obey the boss, to show unquestionable loyalty and devotion, and never to make decisions or solve problems without the approval of the boss. This superior/subordinate situation does not allow employees to develop any degree of self reliance personally or on the job. They are rarely permitted to think for themselves or develop confidence in their abilities. Thus it is unrealistic to expect employees to accept real responsibilities.

Obviously this superior/subordinate relationship in traditional business will not develop the positive qualities that could be released in most employees: the intelligence, self-reliance, and creativity needed to contribute meaningfully to the success of a business.

Individual versus Team

Mexicans at work attach great importance to the individual. Traditionally, superior/subordinate relationships take precedence over the efficient organization of responsibilities. All work is organized along strict hierarchal lines, with delegation taking the form of tasks being assigned to subordinates.

A subordinate feels a personal responsibility and loyalty to the boss, but has little concern laterally, unless a friend is involved. The concept of teamwork, with a sense of mutual responsibility and cooperation between departments and sections, is almost nonexistent and runs contrary to the traditional individualistic values of personal trust and recognition within the hierarchal structure. Trying to shift value judgments to group recognition, performance and planning, and decision making is a major change for a society based on individual loyalties. This constitutes a major change in outlook towards work satisfaction, fulfillment, and performance.

Summary of Cultural Influences

Recognizing Mexico's deep-rooted cultural values is the prerequisite for a successful transition to modern management. The degree to which the executive at work separates deeply held positive values from traditions and habits that require modification depends on a number of different factors. The region of the country where one lives exerts great influence. Areas industrialized for some time, such as the North, are much more open to new ideas and change. Other areas remain traditional in outlook and more resistant to change. Most important of all, however, are executives' leadership qualities, vision, and ability to build and inspire effective team management, without which only superficial changes occur.

Chapter Five

Management Styles Compared

"All American managers need to accept that modern management, Mexican style, is not an exact copy of U.S. modern management. Rather it is an amalgam of managerial influences from the U.S. and other countries adapted to the deeply held Mexican cultural values that give it Mexican identity."

To compare Mexican traditional and modern styles this chapter examines key management concepts: planning; organization and delegation; control and follow-through; evaluation and promotion; training and development; interdepartmental responsibilities; attitudes toward superior position, change, and conflict; and teamwork. This provides the context for comparing Mexican styles to emphasize the opposite ends of the traditional to modern transition continuum. Presently, most Mexican companies are a mix of both styles.

After an overview of traditional/modern Mexican companies, the various concepts are each sketched from the traditional viewpoint and from the modern viewpoint. These are followed with commentary to provide insight for U.S. managers working in Mexico.

Overview

The most traditional Mexican companies are managed from the top by owners who share little information, knowledge, or ideas with subordinate managers. CEOs are dedicated to the profitability of their businesses, as these provide a comfortable living for themselves and family, secure status in their community, and provide a heritage for their children. The outlook is usually local, but in the case of larger companies, regional and national interests are important. Little stress has been placed on competition, quality, delivery of product, or pricing. Customers are cultivated through personal connections and they remain loyal as long as they feel treated well. Explicit company philosophies are not articulated, since the character of the CEOs projects company values and philosophy. Business life is *tranquilo* and dependent upon the boss.

In the most modern Mexican companies, CEOs view themselves as part of a carefully selected management team. They bear responsibility for final decisions, but depend extensively on team members to contribute ideas and opinions to reach well informed decisions. CEOs give priority to developing a clearly articulated company philosophy and culture that provides guidance for everyone working in the company. Company mission statements usually relate to these major areas: 1) overall company purpose—product and service; 2) relationship with the customer; 3) interpersonal relationships; and 4) relationship with and responsibility to the community.

American managers today find that most Mexican companies and managers still operate in a comparatively traditional work environment. Mexican managers, however, are changing rapidly. Sometimes they are traditional in some aspects, while modern in others. How far management in Mexico has progressed in the transition from traditional to modern varies by region, company size, and company type. But more than any other factor, successful transition depends upon the attitude of Mexican CEOs with whom managers have worked.

In the Mexican business environment some culturally sensitive American managers will quickly identify the differences between U.S. and Mexican participative styles. All American managers need to accept that modern management, Mexican style, is not an exact copy of U.S. modern management. Rather it is an amalgam of managerial influences from the U.S. and other countries adapted to the deeply held Mexican cultural values that give it Mexican identity.

Planning

Traditional

In traditional Mexican companies objectives exist in the mind of the owner and rarely are committed to writing. The CEO has plans, but his personal objectives tend to be short term. A typical view is: "How can I plan anything but short term because one never knows what the government might do, such as devaluations, new taxes, or new regulations?" With the cost of borrowing high, the traditionalist plans for quick turnover of capital, large profit margins, and relatively small volumes.

Traditional CEOs rarely consult their management group about objectives or plans. Their responsibility is to do their jobs as assigned without asking too many questions. As employees, without status of ownership or participation, they would feel indiscreet to inquire about the objectives and plans for the company's future. The CEO (or a small number of owners) in a traditional company set plans and priorities. These are viewed as desirable goals, not commitments, so that achievement of them is variable. Failure to achieve objectives is common, and these failures are viewed as unforeseeable due to extenuating circumstances not related to management style.

Modern

In modern Mexican companies CEOs originate plans by drawing up overall company objectives. These are developed and elaborated in detail by the senior management team and recorded in writing. They are categorized into long-, medium-, and short-term objectives, with built in flexibility to allow for unforeseen changes in the economic climate of Mexico. A planned time frame for execution of the objectives is developed, which members of the management team fully commit to achieving. Extensive time is expended in planning every detail to make sure the plan is realistic and achievable.

Insights for U.S. Managers

The transition from traditional to modern planning has been difficult in those Mexican companies attempting it. Most troublesome has been detailed planning because the Mexican tends to be overly optimistic in time estimates and lacks experience with logical step-by-step analysis and planning. Planning has also been problematic because the average CEO and his management have difficulty getting used to living with what has been planned instead of changing direction whenever a problem has occurred.

Most Mexican managers still are accustomed to the fairly short-term, six-year Mexican presidential term-of-office planning guide. Within the context of daily, weekly, or monthly planning, the majority have limited concrete experience or training in detailed planning related directly to objectives. Most need development and training in the process of translating objectives into detailed plans of action, and to commit them to writing in a logical form. Critical action plans require development in most cases due to limited analytical thinking both in schools and previous work experience.

On the other hand, conceptual planning is usually quite well done, but the transfer to the concrete is difficult. Managers tend to be overly optimistic, omitting some details and failing to prioritize. The solutions to these problems are careful guidance and facilitation and a lot of encouragement every step of the way. Experience is showing young Mexican managers to be intelligent and flexible. Once they feel confidence in their relationship with an American counterpart, they begin to participate, have less concern about making mistakes, and show increasing commitment and a sense of urgency. For the first time in their lives they have the experience of planning, controlling, and feeling the satisfaction of total involvement, as well as the responsibility it entails.

Organization and Delegation

Traditional

In traditional Mexican companies CEOs feel they know what to do and organize jobs into different sections such as financial, production, or sales. They delegate responsibility for each section to different managers (but reserve authority for themselves), and the managers in turn break down the sections into related jobs and delegate these to subordinates. Managers feel responsible for their section but know little or nothing about, nor have any interest in, other sections. Communication is one way—top down. Priorities may be stated but plans of action are not detailed. Time frames are viewed as desirable goals, not firm deadlines.

As work progresses and unforeseen problems arise, the boss gets involved to handle a series of crises. Subordinate managers drop everything to attend to the crises, with their work plans and priorities suspended until these end. As this situation repeats itself, original work plans have little meaning. However, when CEOs discuss progress with their managers, they usually blame them for not following 'plans'. They complain that their managers lack knowledge, initiative, or responsibility rather than question problems originating from their own management style.

Managers accept assigned jobs or responsibilities without question, even when they may not agree with timing or the methods of accomplishment.They fear asking for clarification of what is not understood because they do not want to appear uninformed or critical of their boss's decisions. They will try to do their best, but if they absolutely disagree with something, they may do the job partly or not at all.

When the managers delegate their own job responsibilities they tend to use the same one-way communication used by the boss. Priorities defined by them often are forgotten as frequent crises occur. Often employees interpret priority to mean the last job assigned, the pleasant jobs, or the ones the employee likes. They continually seek advice, clarification, approval, and decisions from their immediate boss, who has little time besides handling routine interruptions all day.

Organizationally, a direct line extends from CEO to managers to subordinate employees. Lateral relationships or responsibilities between departments are avoided, resulting in conflicts when cooperation is required between departments. Department managers favor empire building in their section and discourage interference or contact from other departments.

When problems arise in departments, total productivity and efficiency quickly diminish, so that CEOs have to respond to these crises, interpreted by them as interpersonal conflicts rather than symptomatic of personal management style from the top.

Modern

Based on the overall plans and objectives decided upon by the senior management group, members of the senior group become key members of the corresponding middle management team. For example, the senior manager in charge of production becomes a key member of the production management team. In each area meetings are held to plan in detail the implementation of the objectives. Senior managers depend heavily on the experience and knowledge of the middle management group and together they decide on the most effective way to identify and organize necessary activities. Senior managers act as facilitators and guides to ensure that viable decisions are taken, and that interdepartmental coordination and decisions are agreed upon by all concerned.

Senior managers want to support, encourage, and clarify. They realize that the more authority the middle management group is given in planning and organizing objectives, the better the chances to implement them. Senior managers are responsible for developing the middle level managers in all aspects of work and attitudes so that they are motivated and competent to make sound decisions and to work effectively as a team.

Based on the overall plan for their area, middle managers proceed 1) to identify specific goals for their own area, 2) to specify priorities and time frames for intermediate and final goals, and 3) to design detailed plans of action, including quality standards, to attain goals.

Once these steps have been planned, middle managers meet with their own subordinates. They become members of their team in planning their roles and how these will be coordinated. With the middle managers' help they also detail all procedures and quality standards, and discuss possible problems or bottlenecks, including ways to best deal with them. In their capacity as members of the departmental team, managers believe that they must develop and train subordinates so that 1) they have the knowledge and attitudes necessary to function effectively as a team, 2) they are able to make and commit to detailed action plans, and 3) they can establish quality standards to monitor themselves. This assures overall standards and goals down to the lowest organizational levels.

Insights for U.S. Managers

Depending on the teamwork experiences Mexican managers have been exposed to, American managers will need to judge exactly what their concept of teamwork entails. Understanding that Mexicans are concerned about doing a job the way they perceive American managers want it, American managers carry a great responsibility for how they expose their own attitudes and approaches toward organization, delegation, and teamwork. They must carefully develop the participative skills needed by the Mexican managers to bring about the best environment for successful teamwork. The Mexican managers must develop confidence in their own abilities and to trust their American counterparts to feel confident enough to discuss views and ideas that may be different from theirs, but which the Mexican managers feel will work in Mexico. If this does not happen, the Mexicans will try obediently to organize the work and delegate according to their interpretation of the wishes of the American managers even when they feel a more effective way exists.

In this whole process American managers become facilitators. It is vital that they confidently understand how the participative process differs between Mexico and the U.S., and that they have the courage to ask Mexican managers for assistance in understanding the best way to approach their particular situation. Obviously, the circumstances of every company differ somewhat, so that American managers need to be astute in assessing their particular situation.

One frequent problem facing U.S. managers is the Mexican concept of priority. Even though priorities may be clearly agreed upon at the outset, Mexicans will often tend to give priority to a job which their U.S. colleague may bring up during the course of the day. They will usually perceive it as surpassing the previously agreed upon priority. Therefore, U.S. managers must be cautious in how job priorities are handled.

The concept of priority is also related to the Mexican sense of urgency (Spanish has no equivalent word) that U.S. managers will often perceive lacking. This is due greatly to Mexicans' backgrounds, which separate clearly the sense of control and responsibility between the owner (CEO) and the employee (manager). Mexican managers feel a deep sense of urgency to ensure that they have done what they perceive as their own job—they identify with this rather than the consequences of the job on the whole process or indeed the company. These broader consequences pertain to the owners and they must not overstep their bounds. To change Mexican managers from feeling a narrow specific job commitment unconnected to any other management process, to feeling an integrated sense of responsibility for contributing to the management process, is a giant step forward. In Mexico this transformation has occurred only in companies that have implemented a participative system. Only then have managers felt an integral part of the company. No amount of directives, job descriptions, supervision, training, or criticism has worked except for short periods or in rare cases. In other words, a move to real participative management has been the solution, and U.S. managers who recognize this are reaping the benefits.

Control and Follow-Through

Traditional

Traditional Mexican managers delegate tasks to subordinates and feel that they need not check up on those tasks delegated. They know that if problems occur or decisions need to be made they will be told. Moreover, they often feel it demeaning to check on work at a lower level.

Mexican managers also feel that subordinates become uncomfortable when checked on—doesn't the boss have confidence in them? Checking may lead to subordinates' feeling job insecurity, causing stress and unbalancing the harmony of the work environment highly valued by employees.

When things go wrong, one of the following may happen:

1) Subordinates "fix" it using personal resourcefulness, perhaps resulting in a product of lesser quality or higher cost, but pleasing them because they used ingenuity and didn't bother the boss. (As one modern manager said: "We Mexicans are improvisers, that is why things so often go wrong.")
2) Subordinates report it to the boss after the problem has become serious.

In either case employees feel they have done their best. They may admit that they did not fully understand something, but they did not think it necessary to bother the boss. Moreover, they didn't want to present a problem they might correct first, since they want to tell the boss good news, not bad. They have learned to tell the boss only what he wants to hear, so if a problem arises, they may as well wait until it is a real one, since the same scolding is inevitable anyway. Employees inevitably rationalize: "I tried to fix it to the best of my ability," or "I tried my best to get it ready," or "The boss should realize that it wasn't my fault that this other problem came up."

Managers on the other hand become angry and usually blame subordinates for errors when reporting to superiors. They complain that subordinates lack responsibility and they assure superiors that they will reprimand offenders. Managers rarely view their subordinates' work performance as something for which they are responsible. Personal loyalty and willingness to carry out orders, rather than the concept of total accountability for every aspect of the functioning of their department, prevail—an attitude that permeates the hierarchy.

Modern

Modern Mexican managers accept full accountability for everything that happens in their area, including the performance of staff and the achievement of goals. It is in their interest to identify potential problems before they become serious or irreversible, to train subordinates properly, and to motivate them to work well even in their absence. They cannot manage from their offices but must be where the action is: identifying problem areas, helping and encouraging staff, and following up on work in progress.

This attitude pervades every level of management, up to the CEOs, who regularly check on progress with members of management teams and find ways to encourage or assist.

At the manager-worker level, workers soon learn to experience the satisfaction, pleasure, and pride of being involved in exercising their own quality control within their team, and of putting into practice improvements they have developed. In this supportive environment employees are proud to show accomplishments to their boss, are quick to point out potential problems, and are usually able to suggest viable solutions. Employees are motivated because the boss has shown confidence in them as persons and in their ability to work well. They feel unthreatened and have the confidence to share an accurate view of what is happening with the boss.

Managers are careful always to involve their worker teams when discussing plans for their work area. They rely on them for constructive participation, taking their ideas and recommendations seriously. The workers take an active part in making decisions together with the other members of the work team.

Control and follow-through become routine in everyday work, become a practiced form of autocontrol, and become a matter of pride from the worker to the top level of the company.

Insights for U.S. Managers

U.S. managers, totally accustomed to the necessity for control and follow-through, are often frustrated with their initial experiences in Mexico. The experiences of transformed Mexican companies show that resolution of control and follow-through issues is dependent on the extent to which participative management has been developed in the Mexican operation. Once Mexican managers begin to feel in control and responsible for what happens and are committed to the results, they and their team begin to take pride in quality of work. Research shows that this transformation rarely occurs when U.S. companies try to convince Mexican managers that they are personally responsible for controlling what happens in their departments. The cultural explanation for the reaction of the Mexican manager is clear from the previous description. Therefore, U.S. managers must take seriously the limitations involved in transferring U.S. assumptions in management change to Mexico.

Evaluation and Promotion

Traditional

In traditional Mexican companies managers are evaluated for loyalty and unquestioned readiness and ability to do exactly as told. If subordinate managers know the boss well, they know what the boss expects and do it, whether they agree. Key are the personal qualities of loyalty, devotion, honesty, and cooperation. With regard to job performance, key is the ability to perform tasks exactly as assigned. (As a modern Mexican manager said: "In evaluation, the average traditional CEO will choose loyalty over capability.") Evaluated negatively would be independent thinking, especially creative ideas that the boss could not claim his own.

Promotion in the traditional company is based primarily on 1) being a family member or a close friend, or 2) through influence, or 3) by devotion, loyalty, and good performance as viewed by the superior.

Until the present family or friendship connections have assured rapid rise in a company, whether the individual is capable or well qualified—an accepted fact in traditional companies and generally considered normal in Mexican society. This is now changing, and even family members must have some capability.

The second best route to the top is to seek the help of an influential person inside the company or someone in another company with connections to somebody high in the parent company, or someone politically prominent. Personal recommendations of influential persons carry the obligation that the recommended persons perform reasonably well, do not embarrass the influential person who recommended them, and above all, show devotion, respect, and loyalty as expected of them.

Devoted managers with years of faithful service may sometimes be recognized and promoted by a boss. Since this is viewed as a special personal favor from the boss, these subordinates may not make the mistake of expressing the feeling that they earned the promotion. Nor may they now take initiative or make their own decisions. They simply accept their place and appreciate the favor offered.

All three main roads to promotion in the traditional Mexican company rely on personal relationships and influence. Secondary are the employees' qualifications, capabilities, and work performance, although these carry some weight in the second and third cases. Some traditional owners are beginning to recognize that even family members need more education to perform adequately in the more demanding and sophisticated work world of today. Thus owners send sons to university for appropriate advanced degrees. This gives them greater credibility with other managers in the company and satisfies the fathers that the sons are prepared well to succeed them.

Modern

In a modern Mexican company employees' personal goals form the basis for planning their future trajectory within the company hierarchy. They determine the effort, the training and development, and the performance required to move up the promotional ladder. Because managers work closely in a team setting, capabilities to handle teamwork are highlighted and future promotions depend upon overall performance within the group.

Evaluation of managers is divided normally into two parts:

1. Quantitative—referring to performance measured against objectives. This is done as a part of continuous assessment, so is handled as joint meetings between manager and superior.
2. Qualitative—referring to human characteristics connected with ability to work effectively in teams, and development of subordinates to optimum potential—both in performance and job satisfaction. This evaluation involves assessment by peers and subordinates as well as superiors. Companies which have used this approach have found it very revealing and positive.

When managers in modern companies happen to be sons or relatives of the owners, they still must perform well in relation to the other managers. As long as performance remains good, however, these sons or relatives are assured of consistent promotions. Here strong familial influence prevails as long as sons prove themselves, and they will take over when fathers retire.

Insights for U.S. Managers

Evaluation: U.S. managers find that most Mexican managers accept how their boss evaluates them and tend not to comment on an evaluation. The majority of U.S. companies in Mexico have as yet placed most emphasis on performance evaluation related to results measured against objectives, while the qualitative aspects essential for participative management are rarely given much importance. Few companies have introduced peer evaluation or manager evaluation of superiors. The few that have are beginning to understand more fully how they are perceived by the Mexican managers, and this has been helpful in clarifying misunderstandings. The perceptions of the Mexican managers have invariably been different from the intended ones or the self-perceived ones of the U.S. managers. The same situation occurs on the part of the Americans evaluating their Mexican colleagues. As a result, these evaluations have proven valuable in opening the door to deeper perceptions of each others thinking and thus facilitating communications dramatically.

Promotions: Most Mexicans working with U.S. companies in Mexico are pleased with the possibility of having their capabilities and performance being the deciding factors in their promotion potential. Many choose to work with U.S. companies for that reason.

However, with expanded experience of U.S. companies in Mexico, many CEOs are concerned about losing well trained and developed managers to other companies. Salary differentials make some difference in enticing moves, but evidence accumulates that companies with strong participative styles tend to keep these managers. When Mexican managers feel appreciated, are paid fairly, and perceive potential for future development, they prefer not to move to an unknown environment even when offered a little more in salary.

Training and Development

Traditional

Mexican law requires every company to allocate funds for training, and the government checks periodically that companies comply. CEOs, therefore, have training program outlines for managers and shop floor employees. The effectiveness of training or verification of it being conducted is usually not checked, so training often remains on paper—in the realm of good intentions. Even training conducted is largely ineffective, a drain on budgets that produces few tangible returns.

Middle Management: Traditional Mexican CEOs give orders to managers, and they in turn give orders down the hierarchal ladder to the supervisor ordering the workers. The main 'development' function of managers is to make certain that subordinates listen to what is said and carry out orders exactly. Superiors pay little attention to whether orders have been understood and correctly interpreted, and subordinates making errors are considered at fault and censured. Each level of management guards against passing on more knowledge and information than essential, since subordinates should not know too much. Subordinate managers who want to advance, therefore, concentrate more on understanding the personal idiosyncrasies of superiors than gaining access to restricted knowledge.

CEOs are becoming aware that managers need improved management skills, so that many send them to management training courses of some kind. These are usually designed broadly for industrial, commercial, and service companies and tend to be general and theoretical. To benefit from them, participants need to adapt content to their own situations and translate newly gained knowledge into practice—extremely difficult for Mexican managers to do in traditional companies which are unreceptive to innovations that upset traditional top-down control.

Young managers, on the other hand, are receptive and eager to take any type of training. This in itself is regarded an honor, and they can display diplomas received in their office. Nevertheless, they return without presenting a formal report, giving only information to their superior in conversation, and usually evaluating the experience positively. The manager has broadened knowledge, but has no plan to use this knowledge on the job. Those few who try to implement changes based on training come into conflict with traditional CEOs and either abandon the changes willingly or face the serious consequences of overstepping their position.

Workers: Traditionally new workers learned along side experienced ones, somewhat like an apprenticeship without a formal framework. Once the more experienced worker and/or the manager felt the new workers could work independently, they were left on their own, but could access the experienced worker when facing difficulties.

The traditional approach, still common in Mexico, worked reasonably well in the past. But today experienced workers, faced with time pressures, quality demands, and equipment complexity, struggle to cope with learning new procedures which they sometimes resist. Younger workers are more impatient, want to learn quickly, and tend to reject the outlooks and methods of the older experienced workers. Moreover, more young workers enter the work force with technical training and often have more knowledge than older workers. This gap between on-the-job experience and formal technical education creates generational conflicts and complicates the training of new employees by traditional methods.

Mexican managers believe their primary responsibility is for directing and supervising workers, not training them. Training belongs to the training department (if one exists), and it only drains budgets, disrupts production, and produces no tangible results. Their priority is to produce a product, not provide extras.

Since CEOs often echo these sentiments, few traditional companies in Mexico upgrade workers through training. However, recently some have attempted to intensely train new recruits, either through a training department in a large company, or through an experienced worker in a small company.

Modern

CEOs in modern Mexican companies view the development of a strong management team as one of their most important goals. They expend a lot of time and effort on training and development:

1) to share their knowledge of company goals, planning, and strategy,
2) to teach managers techniques to help subordinates develop,
3) to encourage managers to initiate ideas for improvement,
4) to encourage and guide managers when implementing new approaches or innovations,
5) to praise managers for quality work whenever possible,
6) to treat problems and errors as opportunities to search together for solutions, thus encouraging managers to use knowledge and take initiative to formulate good solutions and avoid recurrence of problems,
7) to identify specific strengths and weaknesses of individual managers and to plan jointly with them ways for improving, and
8) to plan the development of existing managers in light of their potential and future manpower needs of the company.

These CEOs view training and development invaluable to the company, an investment of time and money that will result in measurable returns in productivity and profitability. They know that a highly motivated management team is crucial and that failure to develop one fully will result inevitably in the downfall of the company in present day Mexico.

Middle Management: Middle managers provided training and development opportunities are motivated to do their best. When their ideas are taken seriously, they feel appreciated by the boss and their colleagues in the management team and gain confidence that effort will be recognized. They also feel more responsible for the performance of their own subordinates, the effectiveness of their own areas, and the overall image of their company in the business world and the wider community. They understand that their image as viewed by subordinates and colleagues depends on their contribution to the success of the company. Given the cost to the company, managers feel privileged when chosen for outside training and realize they will be expected to apply newly gained knowledge in the company.

Worker Training: Modern Mexican managers realize that new workers enter the company lacking skills and attitudes. They know that their success as managers depends heavily upon their ability to develop and train these workers—their most important resource—and they must be trained to perform to their potential.

New recruits enter rigorous intensive training programs and understand they must perform satisfactorily to be accepted as long-term employees. Once they begin production work, they will be supervised and guided closely at first to ensure that they understand their jobs and exhibit positive attitudes toward their work and the company. Their managers spend time with them on the plant floor (in an industry) and constantly check, encourage, and identify needs that can be fulfilled by training. These needs are discussed at regular team meetings and decisions are made to solve problems that arise. Team leaders will be integral to this process. They can pinpoint workers most in need of help, can talk to workers to understand their opinions and feelings, and can help decide what kind of training would work best to improve skills or attitudes.

Managers believe that properly planned and implemented training pays for itself and more in increased quality and productivity. Training upgrades skills, improves the work environment, and provides job satisfaction.

Insights for U.S. Managers

U.S. managers working in Mexico will be challenged by their responsibility for training and developing Mexican counterparts in modern technologies, processes, and efficient management. This proves difficult because U.S. managers have been slow to recognize how the different way of thinking in Mexico affects the process. Those who recognize and accept differences in Mexico will make progress. Those who complain that Mexican managers "don't understand," or "don't accept," or "refuse to do it as we want it" will struggle. Success has come partially to some managers after long painful periods of work, when the Mexican manager has concluded that the U.S. manager cannot or will not understand them, thus they have to learn the American way. At the same time, these Mexican managers are quick to point out that they can learn and benefit much from the American manager's knowledge, and that is important to the company's success. But they are eternally hopeful that the American manager will become more conscious of their different values and, consequently, respect their different approaches.

Many American training programs introduced into Mexico have created problems and had disappointing results. For the most part, the American companies have been unaware that the design and organization of these programs have been based on a number of American assumptions about participants in training: American education, work experience, and cultural background. Introducing them directly into a Mexican operation is certainly attempting to put square pegs into round holes. Companies recognizing this inappropriate perspective on training in Mexico now screen all training materials planned for use in their Mexican operation. This has improved both the acceptance and assimilation of the training. The key question still is: Who will screen the material? Since Mexico specialists rarely reside in Head Offices, senior Mexican managers have been found in most cases to be ideal for this task.

Interdepartmental Responsibilities

Traditional

In traditional Mexican companies departmental responsibility confers status to managers, who take great pride and accumulate power by building their own little empires with dependent staffs as large as possible. They are little concerned about other managers' departments, shun contact with managers in other areas, brook no interference from other departments, and accept no questioning of their actions by other colleagues—even though they may be creating problems for other areas. When problems become visible, they blame other managers or departments. When they succeed, they feel vindicated in whatever happens.

When interdepartmental contact is necessary, the departmental managers do it personally or under their explicit instructions. In these instances they are careful to defend their actions and decisions, even when these may not be in the best interest of the company—company problems are the responsibility of the CEO. They always feel that they are doing their best within their sphere of responsibility, and recognize that they wield limited real authority since decisions are made at the top. Despite their real limited authority, these managers draw as much as they can from their authority in front of subordinates, who view them as "the authority" and even "the company."

Modern

Modern managers are accustomed to working as team members and fully recognize that close coordination and cooperation between departments brings job satisfaction to managers and staff and contributes to the success of the company. They work with the minimum number of staff needed to fulfill departmental responsibilities, and these staff are trained to work cooperatively and flexibly with staff in other departments.

Modern managers gain status by achieving departmental goals and by contributing to the coordinated goals of the company. They realize that goals are achieved by teamwork at all levels and that departments are interrelated and dependent upon each other for work to proceed efficiently.

When problems arise, modern managers understand the golden rule: Never Blame Others. They realize that problems may occur in any department, and they know that their department will benefit when they help solve problems in other areas. They expect to be helped in return if a problem originates in their own area. As one senior executive of an exemplary modern Mexican company said: "Be humble." He explained that nobody knows everything, so all must be willing to listen to others at any level to learn and improve.

Insights for U.S. Managers

Most Mexican managers find it difficult to break down barriers between departments. The most successful method of overcoming these barriers has been the move toward participative management. This has created the new phenomena of horizontal teamwork, through which managers accept the interconnectedness of processes and mutual support. U.S. managers need to become skillful facilitators to bring about this change and must be deeply committed to the human factor of paramount importance to Mexicans.

Attitudes toward Superiors, Position, Change, and Conflict

Traditional

Superiors: Traditional subordinate managers view their superiors as ones who completely control the progress of the company. They respect their superiors for their better knowledge, their power, and their prestige. Yet they also fear them. They understand that authority emanates from the top and accept delegated responsibilities without question, even when they may not fully understand or agree. They are loyal, try to do their best, and feel embarrassed to ask for clarification when they do not understand something. They will hope for revelation without exposing their "ignorance." They agree to work schedules and deadlines even when they appear unrealistic to them, and hope for understanding from the boss if problems arise or deadlines pass. They will have a good excuse for not succeeding and believe the boss will be satisfied as long as they tried hard.

Subordinate managers understand the importance of informing the boss about progress in their departments, but they carefully select information to conform with the views of superiors and to put them in a most favorable light. Potential problems foreseen are disregarded until they become acute, since their boss should not be bothered unless the problem is one that they cannot handle, and it could go away.

Subordinate managers know that their futures depend upon what their boss thinks of them, thus they try to please him. They expend a lot of energy in understanding the boss's moods and idiosyncrasies and cater to them. This appears to result in more response from the boss than having done a good job. In essence, traditional managers expect bosses to clearly define tasks, to justly reward them for loyal and devoted service, and to waive accountability for the performance of their subordinates. In return they always know their place.

Position: Traditional managers have pride in their position and enjoy status with family, friends, and in the community. They like the power of giving orders to subordinates, and expect strict obedience and servility. They act as father to son when reprimanding subordinates. They always need to save face, so they protect their image and status in all situations and blame external forces or persons for things that go wrong. Traditional managers expect the privileges of their position, such as arriving later than subordinates, taking long lunch breaks, having a personal secretary, and working in a well-appointed office.

Change: Traditional managers worry about change that will affect their status and position, and they resist it. Some leave companies when change is attempted.

Conflict: Managers having disagreements with superiors in traditional companies for whatever reason nearly always defer to the boss, leave voluntarily, or are forced to resign. Subordinate employees having disagreements with managers either will be coerced into doing things the manager's way or forced to leave. This is more difficult to do in unionized companies.

Modern

Superiors: Modern subordinate managers are members of management teams as are their bosses. They appreciate the confidence bosses show in them, their work, their judgment, and their decision making ability. The recognize the heavy burden of accountability for what happens in their area and accept it as a challenge and an opportunity to use abilities to the fullest. They welcome the opportunity to express opinions openly, to have them taken seriously, and to help develop realistic plans of action to which everyone is committed.

Should these subordinate managers commit errors, they feel confident that their superiors will help them solve the problem with what ever resources are needed to avoid recurrence. They also recognize that keeping the boss informed, especially of potential problems, is important and appreciated. They strive to achieve their goals and participate actively on the team to solve overall company problems, since their evaluation and promotion will take this into account.

Modern managers expect bosses to be leaders who communicate long-range vision of the company's goals and aspirations. The boss becomes an example to follow. They also expect the boss to support training and development and to provide support and recognition to themselves and all others on the management team. In turn they place high expectations on themselves and their subordinates.

Position: Modern managers have confidence in their skills and ability to handle management team relationships, and thus try to serve as an example. Position is dependent upon working cooperatively with others, and focus is upon the team and developing subordinates, not position. Modern managers do not expect extra privileges due to position, and are likely to work longer and be stricter in punctuality than subordinates. True privilege is being able to have full opportunity to develop and grow with the company.

Change: Modern managers accept change as necessary and are always on the lookout for ways to do things better. They enjoy the challenge posed by flexible goal setting and by the ability to succeed in spite of a changing environment.

Conflict: Modern managers expect conflicts to arise out of sincere differences of opinions and ideas. Even so, they are committed to working out solutions that satisfy all sides of issues and advance the goals of the company. They are willing to listen to their subordinates and take seriously their opinions and suggestions.

Insights for U.S. Managers

Introducing a modern participative management style transforms traditional Mexican managers' relationships with superiors, as well as their roles with subordinates. Transforming traditionally oriented managers does not come easily, since this may be viewed as an assault on their status with subordinates, colleagues, family, and the community and on their sense of self esteem and self confidence. Their security of "place" in the organization is disrupted and replaced with collective responsibility for self, colleagues, subordinates, superiors, and the company. American counterparts facilitating this change need patience in overcoming resistance to this painful if necessary personal transformation.

Teamwork

Traditional

Teamwork in a traditional company conflicts with the fundamental dependent culture prevailing in the traditional work situations. Traditionalist CEOs have forgotten that working collectively was a pre-industrial component of Mexican culture, which had many of the same characteristics as modern teamwork. It was centered on family cohesion and cooperation. Through time and growth of companies the tendency was for families to maintain control at the top and outside workers hired in the lower levels. These were strongly controlled to maintain the status and power of the owners. Hence an autocratic system developed, and collective characteristics almost completely disappeared. Workers in traditional companies view a job as a necessary evil required to provide for family. Work gives little sense of satisfaction and no one in the company recognizes it as having much worth—thus no one works any more hours than necessary.

Modern

Some modern managers perceive that the tradition of working collectively in pre-industrial Mexican culture can be recovered to advantage. Experienced modern companies find that teamwork has helped to achieve dramatic improvement in quality and productivity and to increase job satisfaction and employee morale.[1]

CEOs relate teamwork to family values understood by all Mexicans. Teamwork creates a sense of close interpersonal relationship, responsibility, and interdependence. It encourages self discipline within the team (family), reducing absenteeism and increasing overall work quality. Modern Mexican managers find that the transition

[1] This topic is discussed in greater depth by José de la Cerda and Francisco Nuñez (op. cit.)

toward consensus decision-making is less difficult than individual decision-making. Group members appreciate the opportunity to be creative, innovative, and resourceful. They accept positive acceptance of the group over individual recognition. Teamwork fosters positive attitudes— such as sense of responsibility, respect for commitment, pride in a job well done, feelings of dignity and worthiness for any job done—that naturally are being passed on to children and to society.

Teamwork has transformed the workplace so that workers feel comradeship with team mates, importance of work, and for the first time, recognition by the company of abilities and opportunity to use them. They enjoy freedom and confidence in decisions and planning, and gain satisfaction from seeing good results. They do not want to be late or to miss work because that would be unfair to work mates. On the whole, they feel a family atmosphere exists at work, a place where all do their best to contribute to common goals.

Insights for U.S. Managers

U.S. managers need to be aware that "teamwork" in the Mexican context is different from the U.S. concept. They need to understand that three key factors make it different: culture, education, and work experience. Teamwork does not come easily to Mexicans because of the dependent culture in the traditional work situation. Understanding this may be difficult, but some U.S. companies have been successful in using teamwork in an effective participative management scheme. Those are the ones which have discovered that it is easier for the American manager to move from their autocratic system to a participative management style, than to an individualistically based accountable style—the most commonly used style of American companies with operations in Mexico.

U.S. managers also need to know that development of teamwork in Mexico has varied by region and by the backgrounds of the Mexican managers involved. Common factors considered important for close attention of U.S. managers are:

1) The CEO's depth of sensitivity and commitment to the human aspect of participative management;
2) The degree of decentralized control in the Mexican operation—the more local control, the greater chance for success;
3) The depth of feeling and interest that the CEO and managers have for Mexico and its people;
4) The level of self-confidence and flexibility displayed by CEOs and managers;
5) The successful previous experience of CEOs and managers as facilitators;
6) The capabilities of CEOs and managers in developing people and their ability to assess training and development needs within a new cultural environment;
7) The acceptance of consensus decision making as essential as opposed to the insistence on democratic "majority rules"; and
8) The acceptance of Mexico as a distinct culture that requires management adaptation for success.

U.S. companies with experience in Mexican operations have found these factors mentioned above directly influence long-term success. Some have achieved financial success without attending to some of these factors, but these have been short term and have depended upon convincing Mexican managers to learn the "American way" as the best solution. Mexican managers in these situations adapt superficially, learn some valuable techniques and work habits, but do not embrace the philosophy as their own. They have learned out of necessity to separate the requirements of work from their cultural values. While common, this situation is not consistent with the goal of long-term viable integration. Many U.S. companies with long-term objectives of doing business in Mexico need to rethink what is required to bring about a successful operation.

Chapter Six

The Transition Process

"... can knowledge and skills learned in the U.S. environment be transferred to the Mexican environment effectively without knowing how culture impacts on management style?"

This chapter analyzes initial steps Mexican companies should consider to begin the transition process from traditional to modern management. It then examines the role of communications and the issue of sensitizing. Each section follows with insights that will help U.S. managers adapt to the Mexican management scene.

First Steps

Mexican companies that have broken the constraints of traditional management provide insights into how other companies may initiate successful change. First and foremost, traditional companies must look outside their own walls. In the case of a manufacturing industry, they must ask key questions, such as: What is the competition doing? What price and quality must be competed against? What market exists for a product? What technology is needed to compete? What does it cost? They must recognize the importance of having the CEO personally review what is happening in other parts of Mexico as well as outside the country. They should visit countries with industries that compete with their product. They should access information on available technology, suppliers, and competitors provided by information services of different governmental agencies and business associations, often free of charge. They should visit trade shows and search for up-to-date published material in the field.

Once the step of doing outside homework has been taken, these companies should look within themselves, following eight other basic steps:

1) Initiate Self-analysis
2) Establish Overall Objectives
3) Develop a Management Team
4) Establish a Company Philosophy
5) Plan Strategically for Specific Goals
6) Develop the Team
7) Implement Control and Follow Through
8) Evaluate Results

Step 1—Self-Analysis

The self-analysis step is difficult, according to experienced executives, because it touches upon long-held attitudes, assumptions, and unvoiced convictions of CEOs and top management that probably need to be modified or completely changed. As one Mexican executive said: "We have many businessmen in Mexico, but few entrepreneurs. Most who call themselves *empresarios* are really *comerciantes.*" Without soul searching, openness, and determination to change on the part of CEOs, to hope for fundamental improvement is futile. The process of self-analysis is often referred to as sensitization, discussed more fully later in this chapter.

This step assesses where the company's management stands at present. It involves analysis of all key departments, such as production, finance, marketing and sales, and human resources. In the past Mexican companies have looked to their financial wizards to keep the company on track. Consequently this sector gained tremendous importance in most organizations. However, many companies now find that they cannot tighten their belts any more and have to shift attention to production and marketing to survive in today's competitive environment. This shift requires fundamental changes in the attitudes of management to focus on efficiency and quality. This makes complete analysis of present management practices and attitudes essential. The exercises reproduced in the Appendix will be found useful for this analysis.

Step 2—Establish Overall Objectives

This entails decisions about long-term company directions, planned products or services, specific objectives desired, and corresponding time frames. These in turn break down into medium and short-term plans and objectives. Initial decisions demand breath of vision, knowledge, and conviction of the owner/CEO, and total commitment and loyalty from the management team.

Step 3—Develop the Senior Management Team

The CEO selects the senior management team with care because it forms the lifeline of the company. Executives selected must be professionally competent and committed to the change the company needs to implement. It is important to represent each key area on the team, since the CEO cannot be an expert in every area. The CEO must also be careful not to override others and impose personal views. If this happens decision making becomes isolated and less informed, potentially reverting to the traditional autocratic approach.

Management team members will not develop automatically. The CEO needs to inspire and provide vision to maximize their capabilities. This needs to be done daily, and is essential to build a solid foundation for modernization.

Step 4—Establish a Company Philosophy

A company philosophy incorporates written basic principles and values to which all agree to subscribe. This will vary among companies, but usually includes statements covering the following:

- Responsibility to and relationship with customers or clients,
- Responsibility to the community and the environment,
- Responsibility to and attitude toward profits and reinvestment, and
- Interpersonal employee/management responsibilities and attitudes within the company.

Once established and written, these may be simplified and rewritten to improve understanding among all employees and to relate them to their daily work and life. It helps to post them clearly in all key working areas to serve as a reminder of the company wide commitments from the CEO to the workers.

Step 5—Strategic Planning for Specific Goals

The management team has key responsibility for planning and coordinating all principal activities decided upon to attain company goals. This is often stated but seldom practiced. In Mexico the process is difficult and time consuming because it requires focusing on several areas unfamiliar to traditional managers, such as:

a. Assuring constant commitment to the agreed upon objectives, in spite of problems that inevitably arise;
b. Combining concrete objectives with realistic time schedules, which requires logical, clear, and detailed planning and eschews over optimism, vagueness, and wishful thinking characteristic of many companies in the past;
c. Providing flexibility and alternate contingency plans to allow for economic or market changes;
d. Translating written plans into purposeful action, taking into account agreed upon priorities, interrelated activities, and interdepartmental coordination;
e. Selecting, developing, and training the next line of subordinates; and
f. Committing to the role of facilitators to lower level management or worker teams.

Step 6—Lower Level Team Development

Each member of the senior management team becomes an organizer, developer, and motivator for the teams developed at the next lower level.[1]

Then lower managers form teams of their subordinates. This sets the stage for the functioning of each department, where systems are decided upon and implemented, interpersonal and interdepartmental relationships are established, and detailed planning for achievement of departmental objectives is done. In this stage of the process the senior management team may need some special training and assistance to learn how to initiate and develop effective teams. When they lack necessary knowledge, major problems at this stage are inevitable and results could be disastrous.

Once teams have been organized, the manager works with each in planning together the details of how they can most effectively organize their activities and implement the systems needed to attain departmental objectives. It needs to be emphasized that the process of change to teamwork is slow, and companies in transition have found that the senior manager has heavy personal responsibility. The senior managers must decide how to initiate changes in an area, and at what pace, based on the response of subordinates. Little by little input will be received from team members, who finally will be doing much of their own area planning, organizing, and problem solving. During this process responsibility, control, and accountability shift from the manager to the subordinate groups, thus shifting decision making and quality assurance to the lowest levels.

Step 7—Control and Follow-through

In the early stages of development the management team spends a lot of time and effort planning, problem solving, and ex-

[1]This cascade effect is discussed in depth by Rensis Rebert in *The Human Organization: Its Management and Value*, New York, McGraw-Hill, 1967.

perimenting to find the best way to obtain desired results. They also encourage and motivate team members to contribute ideas and possible solutions to problems. As time passes and team members begin to work together more effectively, quality control becomes paramount and maintaining quality standards becomes a source of pride for the team—they want to "do it right the first time." Management follow-up shifts to coordination between sections and departments. Emphasis shifts from placing blame to getting to the root of problems and solving them—a total attitude change. As a result control and follow-through become a way of life at all levels and cease to be "someone else's responsibility."

Quality Circles: Successful Mexican companies have found that one of the most effective techniques for ensuring continuous quality control and promoting continuous improvement in processes and product is the formation of some type of quality circle. When well formulated, conscientiously facilitated, and motivated, results with quality circles have been outstanding. Here one sees the importance of employee participation to secure consistent quality and continuous improvement. Many feel it is the key to the question of control, because it takes place at the grass roots, in the initial stages of production or service to the customer.

Step 8—Evaluation of Results

Departmental results usually are divided into two categories:

1) quantifiable results: based on objectives set for the department;
2) qualitative: evaluation of the departmental manager as a manager and developer of people.

Results related to achievement of concrete objectives are viewed as a team effort, even though the department manager bears ultimate responsibility. These evaluations are handled as routine departmental progress reviews to compare performance with agreed upon objectives. They serve as an opportunity to discuss suggestions about how to best improve performance and overcome problems.

The evaluation of the manager as an effective leader, on the other hand, is more subjective and complex, yet considered essential for the successful functioning of any department. The various techniques used by different companies to assess manager leadership mostly include:

a. Evaluation of the manager by peer group,
b. Evaluation of the manager by subordinates,
c. Self- evaluation by the manager, and
d. Evaluation of the manager by superiors.

The main purpose of this type evaluation is to enable a manager to see himself as others see him. Evaluations are considered opportunities for growth and improvement, not forums for criticism and complaint. This openness requires an atmosphere of confidence and trust among all concerned, and often is the time when the manager, together with the superior, discover the root of many problems and misunderstandings.

Insights for U.S. Managers

U.S. companies setting up operations in Mexico or transforming the management of current Mexican operations face problems different from those described for the Mexican company transition process. While U.S. companies come to Mexico for many reasons, cost reduction is a large factor. They come with technology and management know how based on success in a U.S. environment. The big question they face is: How is working in Mexico different? The business will benefit from new knowledge and technology. But can knowledge and skills learned in the U.S. environment be transferred to the Mexican environment effectively without knowing how culture impacts management style? This creates a necessary, if difficult, learning task for the U.S. manager who wants to succeeded in Mexico. The perceptive and open minded ones will tap into their most valuable resource for training—the Mexican managers. Unfortunately, successfully joining these two worlds is thwarted because the importance of culture to management style is underestimated or even ignored, with predictable consequences.

Communication

Communication in management is widely regarded as important and using it effectively undoubtedly has been one of the best motivators of both management and workers. A whole chapter could be devoted to the benefits of good communication and the different forms it takes, but in this book it is discussed from the viewpoint of the CEO, the manager, and the worker.

Communication and the CEO

In traditional Mexican companies communication flow to subordinates is largely one way—downward. To retain all information and control at the top level of the organization, subordinates are told only what is considered essential for performing their function. Subordinates communicate upward only to report periodically and to report problems, usually too late to take remedial action, but not too late to blame others.

Attitudes toward communication have changed in modern Mexican companies, with greater importance attached now to keeping all levels continuously informed of all developments relevant to their areas and to the company. Companies realize increasingly that employees at every level have a keen desire to "know what is happening." This is proving to be key in motivating the work force. The problem posed in a number of modern companies, however, is how to find the most effective means to communicate. Systems adopted vary greatly depending on company size and structure. But objectives are the same: keeping people continuously informed about company policies, plans, achievements, and results of their contributions.

Flow of information and ideas must, of course, include upward as well as downward communication. A major part of the upward flow passes through the different level teams, which feed back useful information and ideas to the management. It is important for the CEO and senior management to keep open a direct lifeline to the lower levels, which cuts across hierarchal lines. One way to achieve this is to have a member of the senior management group attend team meetings at a lower level. Another successful company achieves continuous direct feedback through monthly meetings between the CEO and a senior manager and one different worker representative from each department chosen each month. The representative would openly discuss ideas, suggestions, or problems concerning their departments, enabling the senior manager to gain direct insight into what is happening at the lower levels. The senior manager would be responsible for finding an answer within a specific time to all the questions raised by participants at these meetings. This also allows participants to gain confidence in having their ideas and potential grievances heard at the highest level and to expect answers. To management it provides feedback and alerts them to potential communication blocks between managers and subordinates.

Communication and the Manager

Modern managers spend large proportions of time in communicating with subordinates. This can involve regular team meetings, written communication passed through the team leaders, or person to person contacts. Managers are fully convinced that communication is important.

Modern companies are finding that frequent short meetings with working teams create effective channels of communication. The meetings are usually brief, but planned to make good use of the little time available. Content can cover a wide range of topics, such as work problems, goal reviews, achievements, company policies, personnel policies, benefits, customer orientation, and attitudes. These meetings become a tool for training and transmitting a variety of information.

Other techniques used are training classes, newsletters, bulletin boards, and sometimes full section meetings with a senior manager invited to discuss specific topics. To communicate company philosophy and outlook to employees' families, special meetings and activities are arranged to meet with spouses, parents, and children. These meetings are designed to influence attitudes and habits to enable families to provide a supportive and understanding home environment to company employees. Companies regularly hold family gatherings and the larger ones organize other family events such as sports and classes. A few even offer formal classes in primary and secondary schooling.

Employees at every level like to feel that their job has some significance, that they are respected, and that their work is recognized. In many traditional companies a common comment is: "Nobody cares about me—they never tell me anything, they never ask my opinion." Most employees want to know what is happening in their company: news of changes, improvements, ideas proposed by them and their fellow workers, plans for the future. They want their contributions recognized publicly. Keeping up a steady flow of information has often been confirmed as essential.

Many employees in traditional companies have had years of experience with management saying one thing and doing another. They are understandably skeptical of all communication efforts until they see that management does what it says. This creates trust and confidence. Good communication has a direct effect on inducing positive attitudes. Upper management sets the example and the employees become receptive and strive to meet expectations of superiors as long as they continue to communicate effectively and fulfill their promises. Then employees feel respected, secure, and motivated.

Problems arise in companies when communication is lacking or breaks down. Thus companies must carefully plan a system to communicate at the initial stage of modernization. Poorly conceived or implemented systems will misinterpret or distort information, create insecurity and dissatisfaction that leads to low employee morale, and eventually result in low quality and productivity and increased employee turnover.

Communication and Hierarchal Lines

Strict lines of command and traditional views and attitudes governing relationships between superiors and subordinates impede effective and open communication up and down the hierarchal structure. This blocks two-way communication vital to modern management and total quality systems. Some successful techniques used by different companies to break communication blockages are:

Dress: Some companies have adopted a less formal dress code for the management group to help reduce feelings of separation between levels of management and employees and to reduce inhibitions to communicate upward from subordinate to superior. Others have adopted a company uniform for all employees from CEOs to workers.

Offices: Offices traditionally stand as a symbol for status and thus intimidate subordinates from communicating upward. Companies have attempted to soften this barrier many different ways, such as instituting open door plans to removing offices altogether.

Linguistic Forms of Address: By always addressing superiors in the formal *usted* form in Spanish, subordinates avoided closeness and familiarity in traditional hierarchal structures. One company has had success in improving two-way communication by insisting that superiors and subordinates at each level speak and refer to each other in the familiar *tu* form in Spanish.

Modern management accepts that by whatever means are effective, blockages to upward communication have to be broken down to facilitate open and direct two-way communication at all levels.

Insights for U.S. Managers

Effective communication is directly enhanced to the degree that American and Mexican managers learn to understand each other's mental and emotional makeup and those cultural forces that influence them. While the same language is often applied to situations, perspectives differ related to what has been said and what is done. Having the Mexican manager learn English will not in itself cause misperceptions and misunderstandings to disappear. A typical example of this occurs when a U.S. manager tries to ascertain the status of a particular job. He often feels that he cannot obtain a "straight" answer from his Mexican counterpart, whereas the Mexican manager feels that he has given a perfectly acceptable explanation. Without understanding Mexican culture and knowing how to use that knowledge effectively in management is the root cause of communications problems that frustrate many U.S. managers working in Mexico.

Useful techniques and guidelines found to help U.S. managers to overcome initial management hurdles in Mexico are:

1) **Initial Meetings**: American managers should be low key and encourage Mexican managers to express their views as an initial step in developing confidence and mutual trust. They should display a keen interest early in learning about Mexico and its people. They should encourage the Mexican managers to explain the characteristics of the region, city, and community in which the company is located. This genuine interest will help open the door because the Mexican manager will begin to feel that the U.S. counterpart is sensitive to and interested in aspects of culture that give meaning to positive working relationships. In the process the American manager will gain considerable insight into how Mexicans think and feel, which will prove helpful in related work situations.
2) **Managers' Meetings**: American managers have the tendency to get to the point quickly, are outspoken, and expect others to be the same. Mexican managers are usually conservative and remain silent in meetings until they hear the American managers' views and approaches to different issues—and that typically happens early in the meeting. Once the American has expressed a view, the Mexican is usually asked for an opinion, at which time the Mexican will usually agree diplomatically with the Amer-

ican (considering that after all he represents the company and so one is expected to agree), even though he may have reservations based on personal knowledge of the different environment in Mexico. He will rarely express personal reservations to avoid the appearance of questioning authority or showing lack of respect for the American.

To benefit from the true views of the Mexican managers, the chairman of the meeting must be careful to allow the Mexicans to speak first, beginning with the one least likely to express any opinion, then following with the ones more extroverted. Then the American expresses his views. If this procedure is not followed, the Mexicans will remain silent and not clearly indicate agreement or disagreement with, or acceptance or understanding of, decisions and commitments being made. One often finds out only later when decisions are being implemented.

3) **Day to Day Communication**: These several techniques have proven to help bridge the "perception gap" between Mexican and American managers.

   a) **Reiteration**: Due to inherent language barriers, explanations should be kept as simple as possible, and special attention paid to the logical order of steps to be taken. A good practice is to have the Mexican explain back to the American his perception of what was understood.

   b) **Lists**: Since Mexican managers prefer not to put things into writing and to rely on memory. To assure that they miss nothing, American managers have found it useful to have Mexican managers list jobs and priorities. The Mexicans use short notes to list jobs in logical order and to indicate priorities. This will take patience since most Mexicans will resist putting job commitments in writing. They may feel threatened and interpret this as a way the American plans to catch them more easily in a mistake. Experience has shown, however, that they will come to see the benefit of this approach in their own work, and this method has proven effective for developing critical action path logic.

c) **Blame**: When mistakes occur, Americans tend to go directly to the responsible person to affirm that the mistake is their responsibility to correct. This approach in Mexico, however, may be interpreted as personal criticism so that the first reaction of the Mexican is to save face, since he does not separate personal and work criticism.

   The most successful communication techniques avoid direct confrontation or blame. One effective method is to go to the person involved in a mistake and say something to the effect that "We have a problem with such and such that happened." The Mexican knows that he is at fault and that you know it too, but he cannot voice this without negative reactions. He will probably first blame someone else or another department. The objective of the communication strategy is to diminish the tendency to blame and to concentrate on finding solutions no matter who is at fault. This avoids excessive energy being spent on personal feelings rather than on solving the problem.

d) **Recognition**: Verbal recognition of positive efforts or achievements for even small things should be frequent and public. This can be oral comments or other forms of recognition such as certificates or coffee and cake. Recognition affects both the recipient and coworkers and is known to be an excellent motivational technique that speeds the process of transformation to a participative style. Criticism should be handled privately to avoid negative repercussions.

e) **Progress Graphics**: Charts and other visual displays of progress provide an open and constant picture of performance related to objectives and have been found to increase motivation and feelings of participation, especially when the employees keep the charts and have the opportunity to present and explain results and to challenge the rest of the group.

f) **Suggestion Box**: This old method of communications has been modified to show that the company places great importance on ideas and participation. Some companies give written responses to all suggestions within a specified time and reward people significantly for usable suggestions. Since Mexicans are creative and innovative, this gives them an outlet that will take their ideas seriously. Some Mexican companies that have transformed to a participative style are enjoying significant savings and innovations through employee suggestions.

Sensitization

The Mexican Experience

Changing cultural behavior is always difficult. For executives of companies striving to modernize management approaches, changing traditional culture is of key importance. The time comes when persons have to go through a type of self analysis to examine in a supportive environment present beliefs and behaviors to become sensitized to shortcomings. This is what is referred to as sensitization. Executives following this process become more open to adopting new attitudes toward work, family, interpersonal relationships, outlook on life, and responsibilities in general. These are profound cultural changes; in most countries they have come about in the course of their evolution from an agrarian to an industrial society, usually over a period of several decades. Mexico, however, is in a position where external pressures are extremely powerful and time is a luxury in short supply. Traditional companies are being forced to change and modernize rapidly or face almost certain failure. This change, which Mexico is having to make in one generation, has been equated to that which took Western Europe and the U.S. over four generations to achieve.

Some companies that have used sensitization to help modernize have found that this process has been greatly smoothed and accelerated by using the services of industrial psychologists. This clearly requires a psychologist with excellent knowledge of what constitutes the management function in the type of business involved. Under these circumstances transition has been speedier and deeper and executives have been solidly convinced of the benefits of new approaches to their jobs and life.

Three factors that have influenced the pace and difficulty of sensitization are status of establishment, location of company, and size of company. Older established companies with work forces accustomed to traditional behaviors and attitudes among management have a greater challenge to change than more recently established ones whose work force enters a new environment with flexible attitudes and readiness for change. Companies from the North, where people tend to be less traditional and more accustomed to change, find the transition to modernization less traumatic than companies from the South, where people tend to be more traditional and resistive to change. Not surprisingly, a greater number of companies in the North than in the South have made good headway in the transition process. The transition tends to be more complex the larger the company, although large companies have already made some changes because they are exposed more to international markets. They have more money available to hire professional consultants to assist them, thus they have already put into operation some aspects of the modernization process. Even so, most still feel that they have a long way to go before the transition is complete. Medium and small companies have more severe problems. They are the ones most likely to have been slow to realize that changes are essential for survival. Since they are family owned and traditionally operated, the pressure for rapid and fundamental changes comes as a profound shock. Some are turning operations over to their sons. Some are changing their products or services. Some are trying to make limited structural changes. Some are selling their businesses. Those businesses that plan to carry on will have to have management go through some form of sensitization to prepare for new approaches.

CEOs and upper management find it particularly difficult to accept the need for sensitization. Sometimes they prepare for change by requiring their managers and supervisors to go through sensitization courses, but they feel they do not need it. When this happens, the transition process proceeds poorly or not at all. When CEOs and senior managers perceive that they do not need self-analysis, it is extremely important that they still go through it with an open mind. This makes a big difference because they become sensitized to modern approaches and, more importantly, they set an example for their other employees. They also develop greater understanding and empathy for others by having gone through the process. As one successful CEO stressed: "All employees must see that even the CEO has something new to learn."

Insights for U. S. Managers

U.S. companies with operations in Mexico need to be sensitized to the new roles required of Head Offices. Indeed, in today's global marketplace these Head Offices have had to adjust to the requirements for long-term viability in business. From the viewpoint of progressive companies, some of the major considerations are:

1) **Decentralized Control**: For U.S.–Mexican operations decentralization has meant placing the majority of decision making in the hands of Mexican based general managers. Hence Head Offices must develop a high level of confidence in the people in charge of their Mexican operations.
2) **Long-term Commitment**: Head Offices trying to plan short term in the past created problems. Short-sighted examples have been the attempt to turn a plant around in two years, or to link the American manager's performance and future promotion with his ability to organize a successful Mexican operation in the same time as would be expected in the U.S. Short-term decisions have often prejudiced long-term viability. Companies are learning, with few exceptions, that long-term commitments are essential to be successful in Mexico.

3) **Manager Selection:** Successful Mexican operations, with few exceptions, succeed long term with Mexican general managers and management teams. The American managers selected for Mexican operations in these companies are primarily "training managers" assigned to key positions.They are sent to Mexico to provide training, not to fill a specific position for an unspecified time. They in turn select Mexican counterparts for each position. The job of these American managers, therefore, is to train and develop Mexican managers to take over their respective positions, after which they return home. This normally takes from two to four years.

   Two key characteristics for American managers under these circumstances to be successful are flexibility and sensitivity to other cultures. Learning Spanish well is also important. Sometimes Human Resource experts in the Head Office have assumed that the best candidates are American managers with Mexican cultural heritage. With few exceptions, however, these persons have not worked out well. While they speak Spanish and have strong ties to their Mexican heritage, they are too strongly influenced by their American education and work experience to work effectively as "training managers". They have in fact become "Americanized" in their way of working and thinking about work. As a result they are mostly direct in speech, critical when they see fit, and often offend the sensitivities of the Mexicans who perceive much of their attitude a feeling of superiority. This has created many stressful and sometimes disastrous situations.

4) **Head Office Support Function**: Specialists in the Head Office fulfill an important support function for the Mexican operation that has been decentralized. The Mexican general manager, once overall objectives have been agreed upon for the Mexican operation, is responsible for achieving objectives using whatever style is most successful in the Mexican environment. The Mexican operation assesses what they need from the Head Office.

   In U.S. companies without decentralization, General Managers in the Mexican operation can feel caught between conflicting directives from the Head Office and the realities of working in Mexico. Without direct experience in day-to-day operations in the Mexican operation, Head Office specialists will find it difficult to understand the Mexican operation. As a result mutual frustration and misperception will arise frequently.

5) **New Manager Orientation**: Orientation to working in Mexico, even in border areas, is critical to avoid serious culture shock among American managers assigned to Mexico. This orientation needs to attend to both managerial and cultural issues. It should not be limited to managers being assigned to Mexico, but should extend to Head Office staff who will be supporting the Mexican operation. Initial orientation needs to be followed after three to four months with additional orientation grounded more directly on issues specific to a company and its work environment.

Chapter Seven

Advice to Executives in Transition

> "*U.S. managers should be aware of the factors important to Mexican managers in transition. In addition,...[they need to listen well and ask questions, study Spanish, admit mistakes and acknowledge ideas, accept social contact, avoid criticism of Mexico, and have patience].*"

From a Mexican perspective, this chapter presents practical advice for any executive dealing with the transition process. This advice relates to changes in attitudes and behavior patterns and management practices. It is based upon extensive interviews with modern Mexican executives who eagerly shared what they learned by attempting to modernize.

Maintain a Positive Frame of Mind

When outlining a new approach to managers, CEOs need to avoid the natural tendency to emphasize the obstacles to change. Instead they need to emphasize what is doable and to call upon the natural creativity and resourcefulness of the Mexican managers to find new ways to circumvent old problems.

Learn to Put Plans in Writing

Since Mexican CEOs and managers are used to committing everything to memory, putting plans in writing is difficult. Relying on memory, however, has distinct disadvantages such as forgetting to do something and being unable to organize and think in detail to devise action plans for essential activities. Committing plans to writing forces personnel to examine logically and analytically the order of priority of activities and the coordination needed among sections and departments. Steps are carefully thought through in advance to reduce the chance of forgetting and leaving out important details.

Do Not Shift Blame on Others

The natural inclination of traditional managers is to blame others—subordinates, other departments, or outside uncontrollable forces. While this shifts the problem from the manager's shoulders to those of someone else, it does not effectively address and solve the problem. The traditional manager fails to recognize this.

To overcome this natural inclination, traditional managers first must start to catch themselves beginning to blame others when something goes wrong in their area. Then they must think: "Since the problem is in this area, I am responsible." From this they must follow through and try to determine the cause of the problem and ways to solve it. If it is a problem caused by a subordinate, then a solution can be found in this area. If it is one being caused by another department, then the manager will have to meet with the other manager and try to solve the problem. If the problem originates outside the company, then the manager must try to control it, or at least find a way of overcoming or minimizing its detrimental effects. The key is pursuing a solution to the problem no matter what or where its origins.

Be Humble

CEOS and managers should never pretend to know everything. No human is omniscient. Rather they should listen to other managers and to subordinates and try to learn. Good workers probably know more about the idiosyncrasies of their own jobs than their managers, so it is beneficial to listen to them. They in turn will respect and admire the person who does listen, and be more likely to share information readily. Listening has proven to be one of the most effective ways of stimulating subordinate participation in a company and in developing their full potential as employees.

Managers—Do Not Be Afraid to Say What You Think

Since managers traditionally have been conditioned to be quiet and do as they are told, they find it difficult to all of a sudden open up and speak their minds. Superiors help managers to open up by showing that they regard it important for managers to say what they think without fearing rebuff. This means that superiors must respond to all ideas and suggestions, even if all are not practical or useful. This also means that managers need to learn that what they suggest must be well thought through and workable. When their suggestions are accepted, they must be prepared to commit to achieve measurable results. With open communication comes increased accountability.

Take Time to Train Subordinates

Managers commonly complain that they have no time to train subordinates. Clearly, however, managers cannot afford the luxury of not training them. In a modern company meeting departmental objectives by and large depends upon the manager's ability to train and develop subordinates. Thus training can also assure the manager's success and promotion.

Training is often misperceived as being formal classes. More often, however, it entails daily contact with subordinates with an eye upon assisting and encouraging them and determining first hand their relative strengths and weaknesses. Managers cannot manage from the isolation of their offices, and they usually learn more from frequent brief meetings with subordinates in a team sharing atmosphere than in less frequent but longer formal meetings.

Training sometimes seems wasteful to managers when subordinates do not listen or understand explanations and continue to repeat mistakes or do something entirely different than expected. This can be overcome by recognizing that situations will have both a managerial and a subordinate perspective. Misconceptions often are erased by having subordinates repeat or explain to managers in their own words what they thought was said and expected of them. This also reinforces with the subordinate the steps to be followed to perform an activity.

Initially, managers need to plan to spend a lot of time in training. Once self-discipline begins to permeate every aspect of work, subordinates working in their own teams will gradually take over the daily problem solving and planning so that the manager has more time to devote to long-term planning.

Check, Check, and Check Again

Both CEOs and managers complain about the lack of follow up and control. Since modern management makes managers accountable, they need to accept that they shoulder total responsibility for what happens in their area and that they cannot blame others for what goes wrong. They must also be totally committed and identified with the company.

Initially, CEOs will find that they spend a lot of time checking up on the activities of managers until they know what to do and how to do it. In turn, managers will spend a lot of time with subordinates, helping, encouraging, and checking that they know how to do their jobs well. Over time subordinates learn to work in teams and develop their own system for problem solving and quality control. Finally "doing it right the first time" become the order of the day. At this point managers spend less time on routine supervision and more time on planning and implementing improvements.

Say "No" to Unrealistic Plans

Traditional managers have been conditioned to say nothing when superiors propose unrealistic commitments that certainly cannot be fulfilled. The trap observed by one modern manager is that "The [traditional] Mexican manager often acts on sentiments rather than realities." Modern managers take commitments seriously and have to plan realistically. They are obliged to speak up when proposed targets are unattainable in their departments. They must, of course, be ready to justify their opinions and propose realistic alternatives based on their intimate knowledge of their department. CEOs appreciate and respect managers who are realistic. As one modern manager has observed: "Every action entails risks and opportunities. As managers, we sometimes spend so much time and energy on avoiding 'problems' that we miss opportunities."

Have Empathy with Employees

Both CEOs and managers need to have empathy to be able to work effectively with management groups. Without the ability to put oneself in the place of another, managers are less effective. Understanding and motivation build upon the skill of empathizing with others. Managers either do it naturally or learn it.

You Can Do Something About Turnover

Traditional managers believe that they can do little about turnover. Modern managers view turnover as symptomatic of a management problem and try to assess what is wrong and what can be done to correct the problem. They also examine to what extent their management style may be a contributing factor to turnover. According to recent studies carried out mainly in the north of Mexico, most turnover (and absenteeism) was related to a problem with management. When turnover is high, these areas need to be reexamined:

Recruitment and Selection: Companies that establish consistent guidelines for selecting personnel and provide for in-depth interviewing and testing of candidates have less turnover. As one executive said: "Don't make it too easy to get in—it will also make it easy to leave."

Orientation: Applicants provided realistic and sensitive orientation are likelier to show through attitude whether they are suitable candidates for a position in a company.

Training of New Candidates: Rigorous induction training, supported by caring supervision, has proven effective in giving employees a successful start in a company.

Supervision and Development on the Job: Supervisors share great responsibility for helping new employees to succeed in their jobs, and in many modern companies, turnover is treated as an important factor considered in supervisor evaluation.

Role of the Human Resources Manager: Since the importance of this position is generally underestimated in Mexico, it often is filled by inadequately prepared persons. Modern companies recognize the importance of Human Resources Managers in developing the human resources potential of employees to reduce turnover.

Trained People Are Scarce?—Do Something About It!

Trained personnel in both technical and administrative areas may be scarce in both traditional and modern organizations. This is most acute in the technical areas that require specialized skills to handle modern processes. Technical skills divide into two broad categories: manual and diagnostic skills, combined with methodical work habits required in modern industry, needed by technicians and supervisors;

and theoretical knowledge and analytical skills needed at professional levels. Since professional employees generally also perform management functions, they also need to have had training in administrative skills. An acute shortage of competently trained people in both categories exists in Mexico.

While both traditional and modern CEOs recognize these shortages, they react to them differently. The traditionalists rue the lack of trained personnel and blame problems of quality and productivity on it. They also blame the educational system for inadequate training and lack of concern for the needs of business and industry. Rarely, however, do they dialog with educational institutions to remedy the situation. They also provide little or no in-house technical training because they lack resources or because they have nobody with the requisite technical knowledge.

Modernists, on the other hand, are so conscious of their dependence on the capabilities of their management groups that they are using a number of different approaches to address this problem:

Training Their Own People. While this has proven successful in a number of instances, providing specialized technical training is becoming increasingly difficult.

Widening the Search for Trained Candidates. By recruiting in different areas of the country, companies can find persons with skills that are scarce in a particular region.

Collaboration with Educational Institutions. Companies contact suitable institutions directly to organize special courses and seminars on specific topics of concern to them.

Participation in Community Efforts. Companies use industrial and business chambers to develop closer links with educational institutions to influence the development of programs that produce graduates with professional profiles needed by modern business organizations.

Some of these strategies are overcoming short-term shortages, while others will take more time to bear fruit. Nevertheless, all point the way to actively responding to a serious lack of trained manpower in Mexico.

Know Your Unions

The subject of labor unions has been avoided in this book because it has always been a complex subject in Mexico, more so today with the restructuring that the Mexican labor movement is undergoing. Nevertheless, a few words are in order in this management book.

The type and intensity of union activity varies considerably from one part of Mexico to another. As a result, relations between unions and management are equally varied. While not all companies unionize, most have, and companies need to have a labor relations executive with a profound knowledge of the local unions and their leaders. Since labor legislation and the courts are generally favorable toward the worker, the labor relations executive needs a thorough knowledge of labor law. Above all, however, this person must establish good working relationships with leaders of the union representing the company's workers.

The experiences of companies that have modernized their management style have been positive toward unions. They have had fewer problems than traditional companies. This relates to the degree of job satisfaction fostered by the modern human relations approach, and specifically to the opportunity given workers to air grievances without recourse to union intervention.

Most of the companies interviewed have some or all of their work force unionized. Even so they placed great emphasis on seeing that their work force was contented, productive, and personally fulfilled in their work. Thus no desire existed to create discord within the company. It was pointed out, however, that trouble sometimes arose, not from within the company, but from the vested interests of union leaders fighting among themselves. Such situations admittedly are difficult to control and may require intervention of state and federal authorities. Even under these circumstances, modern Mexican companies have shown themselves more capable to resolves union problems than traditional ones.

Insights for U.S. Managers

U.S. managers should be aware of the twelve factors important to Mexican managers in transition. In addition, these other factors should be considered:

Listen Well and Ask Questions: When working in a new and strange environment, the only way to be accepted quickly and become integrated into the groups is to learn to be a good listener and to ask lots of questions.

Study Spanish: Trying to speak Spanish is more important than speaking it perfectly. Language is a window into the culture and the mentality of the Mexican. Understanding the culture and the people rarely occurs without at least some knowledge and use of Spanish, even when Mexican counterparts speak quite good English. Sensitivity to what is really "Mexican" is difficult to comprehend from English only.

Admit Mistakes and Acknowledge Ideas: Mexican managers often complain that Americans feel only they are right and have all the answers. Americans bring to Mexico superior technical knowledge and management systems, but they also forget that they are working and living in a foreign environment that requires adjustments that they may not have recognized. Recognizing mistakes and acknowledging the Mexicans who have good or better ideas is sure to improve acceptance of the American manager by the Mexicans.

Accept Social Contact: Especially at first American managers need to accept the hospitality and social invitations offered by Mexican managers. They should understand that the invitations show genuine interest in getting to know their American counterparts and their families and a desire to give them the privilege of showing them Mexican culture, food, and music. Most Mexicans are delighted with the friendly and open personal qualities of Americans on these occasions.

American managers who participate in these social activities find themselves integrating rapidly.

Avoid Criticism of Mexico: Just as Americans do not appreciate foreigners criticizing the U.S. or its people when they are guests in the U.S., Mexicans do not appreciate U.S. managers criticizing Mexico. This is viewed in bad taste and lacking respect for the country in which they are guests. Mexicans can and will criticize their own country, but foreigners should not reciprocate unless done so diplomatically. One should always remember that it is difficult anywhere in the world to judge others by one's own yardstick.

Have Patience: Patience is difficult to develop, especially under the pressure of work. But almost every process will take longer in Mexico for a variety of reasons, especially in the beginning. Once a company has been established and good rapport has developed in the management and worker group, many aspects of the work process will gain full productive rhythm. However, certain things will take longer in Mexico and most of these are outside the control of the individual manager or company. Mexico is still a developing country, and certain services and infrastructure problems have to be accepted as part of the challenge of having a business operation in Mexico.

Chapter Eight

Mexican Success Stories

> "*[These seven Mexican companies' stories] ...should sufficiently illustrate the points made in this book.*"

The following seven success stories bring to life some of the outstanding Mexican companies that have succeeded in modernizing management. Some have had almost a decade in the process of transition, accompanied by the introduction of new technologies. Others have begun the process recently, making drastic changes in response to economic pressures. Not all seven have completed the transition process, but all have made considerable progress toward modernization.

The companies represented in this chapter are a select group. Before inviting them to write their stories for *La Administración Mexicana en Transición,* the author made a preliminary selection of companies to assure the reader the greatest possible variety of experiences. The group of seven represents large, medium, and small companies from different geographical regions of Mexico. While all regions could not be represented, this selection should sufficiently illustrate the points made in this book. Moreover, the author researched other companies that have progressed along the path of transition and interviewed their executives. These experiences are reflected in the book but not cited due to limits of length or at the request of the company concerned.

The top executives of the companies, themselves directly involved in the process of change, wrote the stories that follow. This approach was important to preserve authenticity and to allow personal experiences and opinions to show vividly. The companies that contributed their stories are:

I SISTEMA ARGOS, S.A. DE C.V.—Ciudad Juárez, Chihuahua
II GRUPO INDUSTRIAL BIMBO, S.A. DE C.V. —Mexico, D.F.
III INDUSTRIAS COMMONWEALTH, S.A. (GRUPO INFRA)—Mexico, D.F.
IV PIGMENTOS Y OXIDOS, S.A. DE C.V.—Monterrey, Nuevo León
V COMPAÑIA SIDERURGICA DE GUADALAJARA, S.A. DE C.V.—Guadalajara, Jalisco
VI TRANSMISIONES Y EQUIPOS MECANICOS, S.A. DE C.V. —Querétaro, Querétaro
VII VACOR DE MEXICO, S.A. DE C.V.—Guadalajara, Jalisco

Illustration 1. Locations in Mexicoof Successful Companies Cited

I. Sistema Argos, S.A. de C.V.

Origins

SISTEMA ARGOS is a family business originally dedicated to the bottling of soft drinks and the manufacture and distribution of ice. More recently it has entered the field of providing development sites and buildings for *maquiladoras* (in-bond assembly plants) in the border area around Ciudad Juárez.

The group originated in the twenties when the Fernández brothers, together with some other partners, started operations in the ice, soft drinks, brewing, flour, and baking business. In time the business was divided, leaving the Fernández brothers with the ice, soft drinks, and banking endeavors. Banking was relinquished when banks were nationalized in 1982. In 1983 the remaining businesses were integrated into what is now SISTEMA ARGOS, S.A. DE C.V. The present form of the group started in earnest in the 1970s when it dominated the soft drink market in Juárez, with a 95% market share, and acquired a new franchise in Hermosillo, Sonora. This was the first time in the thirty-six years of existence that the group had expanded its marketing horizons. During the remainder of the 70s the company had no other special landmarks, but rapid growth in sales in all its franchises led to larger companies with ever increasing needs for investment and modernization of plants and administration.

In 1983 the company had the opportunity to acquire another franchise in Ciudad Obregón, Sonora, and another in Culiacán, Sinaloa in 1985. From 1972 to 1989 output grew from 4.5 million cases of soft drink to about 42 million. Today soft drink business accounts for 90% of the group's turnover and only during the past three years have plans for expansion of the ice and industrial sites businesses been implemented.

From 1979 to now the present firm has undergone a change from a purely family business to one with a professionally trained management group. This has represented the most significant change in the group. Its consequences are reflected in various operational aspects and in a gradual cultural transition.

A purely family management represents tremendous advantages for a firm operating in a field as competitive as bottling. The success of the firm in the Juárez market has been due, most probably more than anything else, to family management. Decisions concerning investment in marketing could be taken day-to-day by the GM, a partner in the business. On the other hand, the competitor's bottling plant depended on a large industrial group that, to control its divisions, needed complicated and time consuming procedures.

Advantages of family management, however, begin to disappear as a business grows and partners can no longer be close enough to make all routine operational decisions, that increasingly have to be delegated. Defining basic company policies and establishing organization structure that allows responsibilities to be assigned clearly becomes indispensable. Control and information procedures have to be as clear and simple as possible, yet sufficiently complete to compensate for the direct contact of the owner-manager. Besides, it is most important to recognize the need for evolution and growth and, above all, to accept the necessity for support of able and honest professionals. If the owners are conscious of the social role of the company, they will perceive that it is an institution whose existence should not be limited by the life of any one family.

SISTEMA ARGOS recognizes the institutional nature of the company, and over the years we have implemented investment and dividend policies guaranteeing the continuity of the business. Development programs have been implemented that would otherwise not have been thought necessary. Investments have been made in areas far removed from the area of influence of the family, as well as in totally different business lines. All this has been achieved through the collaboration and efforts of an ever increasingly professional management group.

The cultural transition brought about by changes in management and leadership style causes difficulties in businesses that change from purely family to professional management. These difficulties do not depend only on the abilities of the new manager, but have their origin in the inevitably different management styles of the new and old leaders.

In a family business, such as SISTEMA ARGOS was until recently, one commonly finds a close relationship between the owner-manager and subordinate staff and workers. Over many years the leadership does not change and all becomes interconnected in such a way to make everything predictable. This is especially true in countries like Mexico during periods of slow growth, because the demand for workers is low and they remain longer in the same job.

Great affinity between boss and workers creates a great deal of paternalism. Habits form a cultural pattern that continues without change as long as the owner is there. However, as the company grows intermediate management positions need to be created to break traditional relationships. This introduces a new discipline, alters routines, and begins to change company culture.

All these changes must be planned for and the best manner to bring them about must be established. This is particularly true when structural changes involving a person who has held a post for a long time, especially at upper management levels, are concerned. A well thought out plan, well presented in the organization, shows respect for the people involved. Their acceptance implies the acceptance of a probable cultural change.

Finally, in my opinion, businesses that succeed and grow are those that have established long-term objectives. They are the ones that look for permanence and not necessarily high short-term returns.

Matters to be Discussed with Executives of an Organization that Needs to Modernize

1. Learn from Problems, Mistakes, and Conflicts

Problems that arise are solved. What is more important, however, is learning from the experience to design systems that will prevent their recurrence. In addition, this experience should be applied in other areas to prevent potential problems from arising. To act is more productive than to react.

2. Practical Application of New Skills

Make a rule always to apply newly acquired knowledge to real life situations and to evaluate the results in the form of an ongoing practical experiment. Theoretical concepts are thus tested in practice or modified as necessary.

3. Long-term Considerations are Essential

Modernization requires long-term perspective. Executives must not think only a month or a year ahead, but consider implications five years ahead. One needs to identify with the organization and commit to its goals.

4. What Matters is the Way of Thinking

Changing systems is relatively easy. Organizational changes are more complex. Sometimes organizational policies and conflicts have to be dealt with. Training modifies behavior, but what must be changed is the way of thinking.

5. Better Interpersonal Relations

Groups, departments, sections, areas, and others must get to know each other better to learn to think more alike: a common culture that respects individual personalities. We all have different levels of competence. That is not the problem. The problem is how we interrelate. ■

II. Grupo Industrial Bimbo, S.A. de C.V.[1]

Origins

PANIFICACION BIMBO (BIMBO BAKERIES) started operating on December 2, 1945 with one bakery, but its origins date to 1936 when young Lorenzo Servitje had to take over management of the pastry bakery EL MOLINO at the death of his father. By 1941 he had, together with his uncle Jaime Sendra, converted EL MOLINO into the most modern bakery in Mexico. At that time Mr. Alfonso Velazco, technical director of PAN IDEAL, was invited to help with installing new equipment.

Thinking of something larger, Jaime Sendra suggested to Lorenzo the idea of opening a bread bakery for sandwich loaves. At that time these were not widely known in Mexico, but considerable potential seemed to exist for high quality loaves. Young Lorenzo embraced his uncle's ideas and soon after they invited Alfonso Velazco to participate as a partner in the capacity of plant manager. Some time later, Mr. Velazco resigned from PAN IDEAL to devote all his time to the new venture.

Another partner was Mr. Jaime Jorba, Lorenzo's brother-in-law. With his innate gift of salesmanship, he became a pillar of the BIMBO ORGANIZATION. Thus was created the team that soon after founded a new business devoted to the manufacture of sandwich loaves.

In those days the partners used to meet to lay down the basic policies of the firm, summarized as follows:

1. A simple and limited range of products.
2. Scrupulous attention to quality and freshness.
3. Direct daily distribution to the retailer.
4. Effective use of publicity.
5. Permanent technical updating.

Beginnings

There is a firm conviction that Bimbo succeeded because it was not the work of only one person. Rather it is the product of five men, each con-

[1]This account is based on the book *BIMBO: The Story of a Mexican Enterprize*, by Javier Ortiz Tirado Kelly (Grupo Industrial Bimbo, Mexico, 1985).

tributing in a different way: Lorenzo Servitje, Jaime Jorba, Roberto Servitje, and the late Alfonso Velazco and Jaime Sendra.

Lorenzo Servitje, leader of the ORGANIZATION BIMBO, was concerned with the everyday running of the business and was forever looking for the hidden truth and endeavoring to pass on his knowledge to those around him. His great capacity for change, coupled with his deeply rooted convictions, were key factors in the development of the corporate philosophy.

Jaime Sendra contributed the idea. Later, in 1954, he joined BIMBO and worked as head of personnel until 1970. His main contribution was in planning and encouraging the newborn company.

Alfonso Velazco contributed the technology, both with regard to products and their quantity production. He constantly invented new products and he imprinted his high quality standards on the company. Several of the technicians who succeeded Velazco were trained by him.

Jaime Jorba was the salesman—tenacious, hard working, and eminently practical. He developed the firm's distribution methods and handled the ethical training of the sales staff. The driver-salesmen had strict orders never to offer bribes to traffic police to avoid infractions.

Lorenzo Servitje's brother Roberto did not participate as a shareholder in the initial stages of the company, being only 17 at the time. He was, however, the first employee of the company, entering as sales supervisor with a salary of U.S. $12.50 monthly. Gradually, he assumed greater responsibility and finally became Director General, the post he held until March 1990, when he was named Executive President of the Group.

In 1947 BIMBO inaugurated its second plant with five trolley type ovens. Plants No. 3 and No. 4 were inaugurated in 1951. By 1952 BIMBO BAKERIES was baking three product lines: bread, rolls, and cakes and doughnuts.

Over the years BIMBO BAKERIES transformed itself into the BIMBO INDUSTRIAL GROUP, with bakeries in Mexico City, Guadalajara, Monterrey, Irapuato, Querétaro, Hermosillo, Veracruz, Villahermosa, Zamora, Mazatlan, Durango, and Chihuahua. Its variety of products are distributed under the trade marks BIMBO, MARINELA, SUANDY, BARCEL, RICOLINO, TIA ROSA, SUNBEAM, WONDER, PATY LU, CARMEL, and MAQUINDAL.

Policies Contributing to the Success of the Organization

The most significant factors affecting the success of BIMBO can be summarized as follows:

1. The creation of the company by a small group of people whose talents were mutually complementary.
2. The farsighted policies drawn up by the company's founders and, equally important, their rigorous implementation with the aid of clearly laid out objectives and rules of action.
3. A non-instrumental concept of people, leading to harmonious relations with workers and labor unions.
4. A written code of rules governing the conduct of all personnel.
5. Careful attention to the induction of new employees and the continuous upgrading of existing ones.
6. The use, sometime aggressively but always effectively, of all publicity media.
7. Horizontal integration—i.e., the development of related product lines, concentrating on doing what one knew best, but always trying to develop new products and improve the quality of existing ones.
8. Development of suppliers—instead of vertical integration as far as possible.
9. The evolution of a model of 'human organization' through which personnel has a functional participation in its management.

This last point is, perhaps, the most important in the long run. What it implies in practice is a continuous evolution of organizational patterns so as to reflect ever more faithfully the philosophy of the founders: to reconcile the aim of a highly productive organization with a highly human one. This is based on the Christian social doctrine, which seeks harmony between the participants in the production process as an alternative to class war. ORGANIZATION BIMBO has, therefore, been working continually to increase the participation of all its members in running the organization.

The Road to Modernity

The modernization of the company's administrative systems received a strong impulse towards the end of 1962, when the group was restructured. A separate company, CENTRAL IMPULSORA S.A., was formed. In it were vested the property rights to the various trade marks, which were then rented out to the companies of the group. Initially, this company provided corporative coordinating, supervisory, and advisory services, but these were later taken over by DIRECCION CORPORATIVA IMPULSORA, S.C. Similarly, in 1963 PROMOCION DE NEGOCIOS, S.A. was created to control the shares of the different companies. This latter company in 1980 changed its name to GRUPO INDUSTRIAL BIMBO, S.A. DE C.V.

This prepared the ground for a modern business organization that would permit a greater professionalization of services through the separation of line and staff functions. On the other hand, a broader participation of the personnel in the organization was sought in three fields: profits, capital, and management.

Mexican labor legislation provides for the participation of workers in profits. Nevertheless, the Organization has managed to give many of its employees a share in annual profits well above that required by law. The mechanism established for determining, and then making known, the profits subject to distributions involves representatives of unionized and non-unionized labor and has shown itself to be a unifying element for the personnel of the organization.

Capital participation by employees began a little earlier than the corporative restructuring, through the sale of shares of founder shareholders to managers and the most senior workers. Over the years, the policy has been continued to give preferential terms to employees in the acquisition of shares. The ideal would be for all members of the firm to be shareholders, and in fact, the yield obtained by the shares has been highly satisfactory. At present over 10,000 employees are shareholders.

The goal of maximum employee participation in the running of the company is based on the conviction that the employee is not simply an instrument—another resource in the service of the company—but a 'partner' who must be vitally involved in it. And that he can only feel he belongs to it if he, in some way, takes part in the decisions that affect it.

The principal instrument to bring about functional participation has been organization based on teams, following the 'hinge' type of organizational chart. Ever since 1963 each plant has had a management team, generally made up of the general managers and the chiefs of sales, production, finance, purchasing, and personnel. All the members of this team have felt jointly responsible with the general manager for all matters affecting the functioning of the plant. They communicate intensively among themselves.

The managers who were members of this team headed their respective area teams. For example, the production managers formed a team with the chief of maintenance and the supervisors of the different production areas, each of which would in turn form a team with his senior workers or charge hands, who would in turn form teams with their operatives. The linking of these teams has made for easy vertical communication, both up and down the line, as well as provided a framework for horizontal communication.

The principal difficulties found while implementing the policy of participation were due to many chiefs [2] not seeing the need for it, or simply because their staff relations were habitually authoritarian. The element which the BIMBO ORGANIZATION considers the most essential in furthering the humanization of the company and effecting the functional participation of its employees is the careful selection and training of its chiefs. This company is convinced that an organization is only worth as much as its personnel, and this in its turn depends entirely on the quality of its chiefs.

Writes Lorenzo Servitje:[3]

"The task of the leader is to make the objective visible and desirable, and only in a secondary way to trace out the means. This is indispensable. If he orders a certain action, provides the means and the outcome is successful, the merit will be the leader's; the follower will have been an instrument, he will have no merit, and he will be dissatisfied."

...Those of us who are chiefs must be convinced that things won't happen, that the objectives will not be attained, unless the subordinates want them to, when the objectives pursued are their own, when on achieving success they are satisfied because the success is their own."

ORGANIZACION BIMBO was not exempt from the economic crises of the 80s. If it was able to survive, this was, in the opinion of Santiago Castro, the new Director General of ORGANIZACION BIMBO, due to three factors:

1) a permanent stimulus to productivity, achieved by means of several highly successful campaigns;
2) the application of common sense—i.e., not yielding to the temptation of contracting apparently 'cheap' dollar debts; and

[2]Chiefs is understood to mean anybody down from the D.G. to the master baker or section charge hand, who is usually a unionized worker.

[3]"Reflexiones y Comentarios de un Dirigente de Empresa," Mexico 1984, Ed. Limusa, S.A.

3) the good use of lessons learned in the 1976 crisis.

One of the most interesting experiences in employee participation was obtained in PRODUCTOS MARINELA. The aim was to "awaken the interest in contributing ideas by means of a financial reward where, once these were put into effect, they brought about a real benefit to the operation's productivity." The participation achieved was terrific: of over 1,000 ideas submitted for evaluation, only 248 were rejected. The imagination of the employees was fired and as a result "it surpassed the goal set, not only in the number of participants and ideas submitted, but also in the economies generated."

On a poster displayed in the factories and offices (the whole of which cannot be reproduced here for lack of space), Roberto Servitje explained the following:

PRODUCTIVITY, TODAY MORE THAN EVER

First of all we must understand what is productivity.

Some think it is working more...others think it means working harder or more quickly. In total, they think productivity requires greater effort.

Productivity is quite the contrary: it is a matter of achieving the same with less effort, less waste, less cost.

Productivity is working more intelligently, not harder.

The philosophy of ORGANIZACION BIMBO demands a constant search for improvement. The four areas considered priority in this sense are:

- Productivity,
- Quality,
- Participation, and
- New Technologies.

According to Roberto Servitje, the plan started in 1985 has the objective to:

"...strengthen [these elements], promote them, give them impulse and aim for the degree of excellence. These four elements should be synergistic, with no element missing. The four [together] should generate greater dynamism!"

During the last few years the GROUP has put all its efforts into a Total Quality plan which, though it has not been easy, is gradually permeating all levels, bringing about a real transformation that could justly be called"cultural change."

The division of the GROUP into the organizations BIMBO, BARCEL, and CARMEL, which has permitted an almost complete decentralization of operations, has given excellent results.

For 1989–1992 a very ambitious plan has been initiated, already 33% completed, that foresees extensions, reconversions, and new plants, with a total investment of about $380 million U.S. dollars. Four of these projects—MARINELA-TIA ROSA in Monterrey, N.L.; MARINELA-TIA ROSA in Mexicali, B.C.; BIMBO in San Luis Potosi; and BIMBO DE ORIENTE in Puebla—are due to be operation by the end of 1990.

In Guatemala the GROUP acquired a small cake and pastry plant and plans to open a bread plant in the near future.

Important reconversions are nearing completion in MARINELA-MEXICO, BIMBO DE OCCIDENTE (Guadalajara), and WONDER-MEXICO. A strong impulse is also being given to our export drive. ■

III. Industrias Commonwealth, S.A. de C.V.

The First Steps

INDUSTRIAS COMMONWEALTH is a company of the INFRA group, specializing in the manufacture and marketing of industrial gases. It has a work force of 300 salaried and hourly paid workers. In 1981 the company embarked on a complete transformation of its internal culture, as a response to the atmosphere of tension prevailing between the workers, the unions, and the company. This process involved everybody at every level in an effort that significantly improved our relations.

It was decided that the first objective should be a "rapprochement" or drawing together of the firm with the worker's family. For this purpose, the "Family Integration Plan" was drawn up, which fostered a real solidarity (or sense of belonging together) through common leisure activities and creative pursuits. This gave recognition to the workers' daily efforts in the presence of their families, and support to the family through prizes to the children for good school grades and to the wives for their participation in company sponsored courses and other activities. The "integration" thus stressed the satisfaction of success as a fruit of family effort.

"The Winds are Favorable, Let Us Keep on Course"

In 1984, encouraged by the great improvement in company and worker relations, the "Productive Integration Plan" was put into effect. This has already been tried out in our subsidiaries METALOIDES and SMITH'S, where the collaboration between the management team of INDUSTRIAS COMMONWEALTH and external consultants brought about the following results:

- The establishment of interdepartmental objectives, involving all company personnel, because they know them and participate in drawing them up, and which draw together all the personnel, including General and Area Management. The use of a common company uniform (by all personnel from the G.M. down) reinforces the feeling that we are all one team.
- The putting into effect of a productivity program which transformed the worker's attitude by getting rid of the common "That's good enough" attitude through the adoption of clear and firm objectives, such as "doing it right the first time."

"Let's Work Together, We Are One Team"

The Area Managers visited each department on each shift and, with the aim of achieving total participation, the objectives of the Productive Integration Plan were established jointly between workers and managers. As a result, in the first great general assembly of 1984 they committed collaboration of each and all the members of the new team.

"We Must Get Closer to One Another, Let Us Get Rid of the Barriers."

To bring about a closer interrelation between the members of the working team and thus improving productivity, it was decided in 1985 to introduce Gestalt Sensitization Workshops. Up to now, 90% of the company's personnel have taken part in these. The key element of these workshops is to squarely place the person as the organization's most valuable resource, and to promote the rapprochement between group members and the breakdown of interpersonal barriers.

Quality Circles

Guided by the principle that "no-one knows more about the job than the one who does it," we organized, also in 1985, Quality Circles as part of the "Integral Project of Participative Management," starting with a pilot group from the Production Department. Within six months we had six quality circles operating and by 1986 the whole company was organized in 28 quality circles. Each quality circle works on its own initiative, with weekly work meetings during which the workers contribute ideas for the achievement of common objectives, so as to increase quality, productivity, and safety.

The most gratifying result is the climate of cordiality in the workplace and the spirit of collaboration, dedication, responsibility, and genuine love for the work and our workers.

New Proposals, Better Results

The progress achieved presented us with new challenges, thus we declared 1988 the Year of Quality, since achieving the highest quality for our products, based on the quality of our work, is the fundamental objective of INDUSTRIAS COMMONWEALTH.

Recognizing the need to give greater depth to our training efforts, we gave a 12 month Organizational Development (O.D.) course that year. As an extension to the Infra group, inter-company work teams were formed, culminating in a seminar led by the team members themselves. In this way Infra provided an opportunity for members of the different companies to work in joint teams, while in INDUSTRIAS COMMONWEALTH it became accepted that O.D. is everybody's responsibility.

The Road to Excellence

During 1987 Infra started its Excellence Program. The program was presented at a meeting at which were present Mr. Elmer Franco as adviser, the area managers and, as a guest, Mr. Abel Hurtado, General Manager of INDUSTRIAS COMMONWEALTH, in recognition of the outstanding progress achieved by this company.

"Excellence" in Industrias Commonwealth

In November 1987 a committee was formed to discuss the application of the Excellence Program in INDUSTRIAS COMMONWEALTH. The radical difference between the method followed by other companies of the INFRA GROUP and INDUSTRIAS COMMONWEALTH is that in this company the program is implemented by 100% of the personnel, all within 30 days.

The most effective vehicle to implement the Excellence Program was undoubtedly the Quality Circles, accompanied by the design of an attractive and practical work book. Once the program was under way, one can say that the most significant contribution made by INDUSTRIAS COMMONWEALTH was in the adaptation of the plan of action that had been worked out to the environment and realities experienced by the workers, based on the following principles:

- Innovating in conjunction with the customer,
- Giving real and visible service, and
- Offering real and visible quality.

Benefit to the Company, Benefit to the Worker

Today all the Quality Circles in INDUSTRIAS COMMONWEALTH maintain contact with the external customers. Likewise, they are in constant contact with their internal customers, which are the different departments of the firm, given that they provide each other with certain services classified in order of importance.

In meetings with the main customers we listen to their complaints and suggestions, and then carefully analyze them to improve the service provided. All decisions reached carry the full commitment of each Q.C. and department to carry out the actions necessary to give an immediate improvement in service.

The contacts established between departments provide a vehicle for feedback that has permitted the formation of a real chain of customers and suppliers. These work together in harmony, assuming joint responsibility for the fulfillment of the commitments undertaken.

At the end of 1988, at the Annual General Meeting, the Q.C.s reported on the results of the Excellence Program, quoting the achievement as a percentage of the target figure of 100:

- Productivity 169
- Quality 147
- Safety 152
- Service 129
- Operations 172

In 1989 GRUPO INFRA, on the advice of our Management Consultant Elmer Franco, embarked on a Total Quality process and named the General Manager of our company, Mr. Abel Hurtado, to be Director for Total Quality of the groups and to direct the process. INDUSTRIAS COMMONWEALTH viewed this appointment as an act of homage to the daily efforts of our best men and women, employees and workers in the company, proud to be members of GRUPO INFRA.

Everything that implies a change brings with it a certain, and sometimes much, discomfort. In INDUSTRIAS COMMONWEALTH the evolutionary change has been gradual. In fact, our first program (Family Integration) started out with only a few workers and their families. But little by little their number increased in the measure that the genuine interest of the company in its workers became evident. It is precisely this which conquers incredulity and skepticism, and even achieves the active participation of all. Follow up and perseverance see to it that these processes become permanent and continue evolving.

Summary of Organizational Development Program

1981	Family Integration Plan
1984	Productive Integration Plan
	• Interdepartmental Objectives
	• Productivity Program
1985	Gestalt Sensitization Workshops
	Quality Circles
	• Integral Participative Management Project
1987	Excellence Program
1988	Quality Year
1989	Excellence
1990	Total Quality

IV. Pigmentos y Oxidos, S.A. de C.V.

Brief History of the Company

The company now called PYOSA had its beginnings in 1930 under the name of CONVERTIBLES MONTERREY, S.A. DE R.L. The products it marketed were litharge (yellow lead oxide) and Convert Fruit Salt, a patent medicine. Its founders were the brothers Rafael and Julio Fernández Saldaña. The descendants of the former participated actively in the development of the company, one of them (Alberto Fernández) being the present Director of PYOSA. It should not be forgotten, however, that other people have also made great contributions to the company, both in the field of technology and in the areas of philosophy and humanity. Among the first of these must be mentioned Samuel González González in the area of lead oxides and Erick Simon Lehemann in the area of organic pigments.

Currently PYOSA is one of the largest chemical industries of Mexico and competes successfully in both home and foreign markets with such multinational giants as BAYER, CIBA-GEIGY, SANDOZ, HOECHST, ICI, and DUPONT. Its product lines cover a wide range of inorganic and organic pigments, insecticides, herbicides, and pharmaceutical products. This position was conquered thanks to a constant struggle to maintain a quality to international standards, together with the high productivity of all its personnel and an in-house developed technology.

The Most Important Changes Made, Their Implementation and Results

From the technological viewpoint, the most important developments were:

> Operations started in 1940 with the manufacture of lead oxides. This experience made it possible for us to enter the field of agricultural insecticides, due to contacts with potential customers. Pigment production began in 1950, and in the mid-50s dye manufacture began. The range of industrial coloring agents was completed in 1960 with the manufacture of colors for ceramics.
>
> The technological development of PYOSA is the product of the efforts of its personnel. The fact that the technology is not bought but developed by us fills us with a certain pride, as it is rare to

> find a chemical manufacturing company in Mexico that develops its own technology. Besides, in the last 20 years, the range of products mentioned above has grown considerably. It could be said that it was rounded off in the 80s with the manufacture of herbicides, fungicides, and insecticides. The manufacture of these products requires sophisticated technology normally available only from multinational corporations.

Our company owes its technological development to its human quality. I consider that this is the result of the respect shown for our people and a sense of involvement at every stage of manufacture.

The organizational development of PYOSA has also been noteworthy. As a result of a year-long process, we identified around 1982 what we call our "organizational values," which have been accepted by all company personnel as characterizing the essence of the company:

1) Its People are Important to PYOSA.
2) There is Stability of Employment.
3) There is Opportunity for Development.
4) We Develop Our Own Technology.
5) We Have a Participative Management.
6) We Attach Importance to Our Clients and Their Convenience.

It should be said that in PYOSA we have managed to put into effect an organizational language that profoundly affects the decision making process. This rests on the principle of participative management, which dictates our operational style. The term participative management is derived from a process begun 13 years ago, when we learned to find solutions on the basis of people's opinions, and to always seek a consensual agreement, meaning that all the members of the group had to be fully convinced. Our experience has also taught us the formula: "The longer the gestation, the quicker the implementation." Planning plays a very important role in this type of organization. The time spent in the process is unimportant, since it is part of the learning process. We are maturing all the time.

We use models to help us conceptualize some of the problems of marketing, production, and human resources. To mention but a few, we have been helped by the theory of McKenzie, which speaks of two levels united by a superior goal. The first level concerns aspects such as strategy, systems, and structure, which is similar to that which in computer systems is called hardware. The second level concerns aspects such as style, ability, and people. Following the analogy with computer systems would represent software. This model has shown itself very useful in the analysis of management systems. Another model we use is the BCG, based on three points: Belief, Strategy, and Action. These must be focused to create competitive advantage.

It would be difficult for these models to be so richly descriptive to mirror real life processes, such as the impact produced on people by the implementation of processes of change. But it has to be stressed that the participative model, McKenzie, and BCG have become our organizational language and reflect all the theory behind our diagrams, tables, and rules of the game.

In the area of administration, we use a system called MRP II—Manufacturing Resources Planning. Among the several levels of MRP II, we are considered on level A, the highest attainable. This process is fairly recent—3 years—and all personnel in the organization have been trained and continue to be trained in this field and in the fields of organizational theories described above. MRP II includes a firmly structured educational process, supported by a complete kit of training material.

We have found it most important to make our mission fully understood by all personnel. To achieve this we have devised a system that reinforces behavior at all levels: organizational area, department, and individual. Like a thread binding us all together, it assures we all have the same objective and that our mission is fulfilled with the total commitment of all involved. The above system is known as SIFOCE, which is a formal communication system.

Development is very important to us, while evaluations are much less so. We have developed a culture of not thinking of evaluations, but instead of learning the value of developing ourselves; the other comes as a consequence. At present we are working intensively to introduce a total quality system. To advance this process we have assembled a staff unit specially for this purpose, supported by the leading consultants in the field. We attach great importance to this process, since to us quality means culture.

In PYOSA the development of computer systems is a virus that has invaded all departments. Some 95% of administrative operations are computer supported. We even have a channel of the Morelos satellite, giving us direct voice (and shortly image) communication with Mexico City, where the greater part of our commercial operations are concentrated. Our commercial office there employs 100 persons whose function is to satisfy our customers. This sounds easy, but a whole program has been designed to increase the sensitivity of the commercial staff to the needs of our customers. This program goes by the name of SISC, meaning Integral System for Service to the Customer. This is provided with computer support, which breaks new ground in our product area where similar systems are only to be found in the most highly developed countries.

The Most Difficult Changes and Obstacles Encountered

The implementation of the aforementioned changes has been extremely difficult, partly due to resistance to change, but above all due to the difficulty of achieving a sense of commitment by the personnel to the organization, its objectives, and its development. Some of the problems we still have not been able to solve fully are problems of attitudes, in which time plays a very important role. Time is needed first to develop a consciousness and then to go on to make whatever attitude change is necessary.

In Mexico the prevailing attitude of avoiding commitment to anything presents an obstacle difficult to overcome. As we have seen above, we have devised processes in PYOSA that are being implemented with that end in view. Another change that has been equally difficult has been to foster an attitude of understanding for the needs of customers.

Recommendations

- Constantly bear in mind the value of continuous training—and it must be the most up-to-date—for our personnel.
- Have a clear concept of International Quality—i.e., products competitive with those that can be obtained outside Mexico and which satisfy a need.
- Have advanced communication systems, such as computer systems and O.D.
- Have a vanguard vision of the company's product line, to develop products employing the latest technology such as biotechnology.
- Provide goods and services with environmental considerations in mind. ■

V. Compañia Siderurgica de Guadalajara

Brief History of the Company

In the mid 60s a group of Guadalajara businessmen conceived the idea of establishing a steel mill in the city, since a great demand existed in the building industry for sheet steel, rolled steel joists, and reinforcing rods. The idea turned into reality on May 15, 1967, with the establishment of the company. On May 1, 1970, the collective agreement with the Steelworkers Union of the State of Jalisco came into effect.

That same year C.S.G. started production with an installed annual capacity of 50,000 tonnes (metric tons) of steel. Later with the installation of a new smelter and reheating furnaces, output was doubled, accompanied by greater diversity of finished products. In response to the growing demand at home and abroad, the company decided to introduce the latest technology, and in 1978 production reached 200,000 tonnes.

Conscious of the problem of atmospheric pollution, the company installed smoke and dust collectors, drastically reducing residual pollutants. Further expansion of the plant brought installed capacity to 300,000 tonnes.

The Most Important Changes

1) Equipment and Production Systems

Almost from the time of its founding, the company laid down a policy of "continuous modernization of equipment and production systems." This was based on the belief that competitive advantage in this type of industry depends on the quality and cost of the product. Consequently, the company has made substantial investments in this area as outlined below:

a) Installation of an electric furnace with a smelting capacity of 55 tonnes.

b) Installation of a rotary turret to speed up and make continuous the production of steel billets.

c) Installation of a modern rolling mill for commercial products (light sections) with a capacity of over 120,000 tonnes per annum.

d) Installation of a modern cold drawing plant for processing special steels for the engineering and automotive industries.

These investments responded to the following circumstances and demands:

- Inability to satisfy the home market for commercial and special products.
- To compete with the large Mexican steelworks, whose conversion costs are above the international average.
- To compete in the international market, thus reducing our dependence on the ups and downs of the Mexican economy and allowing us to grow more stably and continuously.
- During 1990 and 1991 new investments are foreseen that will permit us to further reduce cost and, at the same time, broaden our product range for the Mexican and export markets.

After almost 20 years, this investment policy has enabled our company to achieve a capacity of 300,000 tonnes of finished products in 1989, and to supply the markets of Mexico, North America, South and Central America, and Europe. It has permitted us to diversify with products of higher added value, such as:

- forged steels balls (for the mining industry),
- special steels (mainly for engineering industry), and
- rolled steel joists (modern construction industry).

2) Data Processing Equipment and Systems

In 1984 we set out to decentralize our data processing functions, involving the following steps:

a) Give this activity more importance, which involved introducing a new reporting level. The unit responsible, previously within the Department of the Controller, was made to report straight to the Managing Director.

b) A program was introduced to decentralize data entry to the departments or units that generated them. Presently the company has more than 35 work stations distributed throughout the organization.

c) The role of the area was gradually changed from processing to promoting information.

This has permitted more flexibility in growth and greater autonomy for the Programmer. The user therefore participates more actively in processing the data. On the other hand, we have achieved an informatics department adapted to the needs of the organization rather than making the organization adapt itself to the needs of the informatics department. Finally, we believe we have significantly improved our internal control systems and our decision making processes. All this was accomplished by the modernization of the computer hardware, to the extent that during the last 6 years we have renewed our equipment three times.

3) Management Systems and Procedures

During 1985 and 1986 we noticed a great need to improve our management procedures, basically planning, organization, direction, and control. Operating and reacting were our strong points. Nevertheless, the new needs of the organization and the requirements of the (economic and political) environment made us feel a need for considerable changes in outlook. To achieve this we made a plan and designed a process of change which meant:

a) Defining, forming, and developing a senior management work team.

b) Reorganizing and greatly improving internal communication practices—among other things, substituting the written memorandum for face-to-face communication.

c) Planning and instituting various weekly and monthly meetings, all with previously drawn agenda and specific objectives to be achieved in each meeting, the most noteworthy being:

- Weekly meetings for planning, production, sales, and bill collection.
- Monthly follow up meetings to evaluate fulfillment and deviation with regard to objectives in the areas of sales, prices, shipments, output, turnover and absenteeism, accidents, bill collection, cash flow, and profits.

The above meetings were focused on planning and controlling day-to-day operations. In addition longer-term planning was catered for by:

d) Introducing a long-term planning model that addresses the following issues:

- Mission and operation philosophy of the company.
- Definition of the business.
- Analysis and evaluation of opportunities, dangers, and strengths and weaknesses.
- Outlining directives for future fiscal years: such as return on investments, sales, profits, proforma balance.
- Establishing and negotiating functional objectives.
- Action plans and budgets.

The above measures have brought about a substantial narrowing of the gap between objectives and actual performance. The deviations vary between +/- 5%, which we consider acceptable.

Products/Markets

With the aim of marketing better products, catering to the new demands of the market, we have broadened the range of products:

a) A greater number of commercial products (light section)

b) Greater value added (forged steel balls, special steels, and R.S.J.s)

The new investments will allow us to expand the output of products such as flat strip and rods.

Diversification

In the interest of continued growth, C.S.G. since 1987 has invested in new fields. This was so in the case of ALUMINIO CONESA and ESTRAL. Both firms allow C.S.G. to diversify healthily in product lines many of which are synergistic or complementary, providing options helping to maintain an equilibrium in a changing market. ESTRAL manufactures storage systems, using steel as its raw material.

Comments on the Most Difficult Changes and the Obstacles Encountered

The Most Difficult Changes:

1) Establishing and committing oneself to a philosophy of operation, both on the part of executives and subordinates.
2) Achieving reliable congruency between the company philosophy and actual practices.
3) Simplifying systems, procedures, and structures.
4) Delegating systematically, measuring results, and using indices of efficiency and productivity.
5) Developing the orientation to evaluate performance by results.
6) Defining the nature of our business and to communicate it effectively to all concerned.

Obstacles Encountered:

1) The executives' great preoccupation with the status a position gives them or could give them, coupled with the great effort

made to preserve it. All this instead of directing their preoccupations and efforts to obtaining results.

2) The dependence of the executive on the Managing Director (paternalistic image).
3) Difficulty in working together in horizontal relationships and teamwork.
4) Fear of participation with responsibility and commitment.
5) Lack of training in the field of the organization and management of human resources.
6) A fatalistic outlook and the constant expectation that others or something will solve their problems.
7) Improvisation.
8) Little or no skill in communication.

Advice and Recommendations for Companies Wishing to Make the Transition to a Modern Management Approach

1) Define and spread through the company the commitment to a philosophy of action (such as concerning the business, customers, suppliers, employees, government) in a clear and simple manner, so that it may serve as a true guide to action.
2) Constantly gauge actions against philosophy and analyze the deviations so as to be able to suggest new ways and strategies.
3) Make strong investments in training.
4) Put into place an administrative operating system that enables executives and employees to measure the results of their actions from day to day. In other words, translate the plans into daily, weekly, monthly, and annual objectives and activities.
5) Detect those who participate in a responsible manner and channel them into the different working groups.
6) When delegating, gradually allow people to experiment and make mistakes, and stimulate the process.
7) Promote rituals and symbols that reinforce the company's philosophy.
8) The top management has to provide leadership through continuously promoting and supporting the process.
9) Whenever necessary, change or remove executives who are putting a break on change. ■

VI. Transmisiones y Equipos Mecánicos S.A. de C.V.

A Brief History of the Company

TRANSMISIONES Y EQUIPOS MECANICOS—TREMEC was founded in 1964 under the protection of the Decree for the Development of the Mexican Automotive Industry, which offered manufacturers of motor vehicles and components incentives in the form of high customs duties on imports and certificates for tax rebates to exporters. During it first year of operation in 1965, TREMEC produced 70,000 gearboxes for rear wheel drive cars and light trucks.

TREMEC started out as a joint venture between a strong group of Mexican investors and a U.S. company that provided the technology. During the following years the company grew along with the domestic automobile market, and in 1971 started exporting to the United States. This started the company on a course of continuous growth which increased production to 500,000 units by 1979, 60% of which were exported and 40% were sold in the home market. TREMEC had over 6,500 employees, 100,000 square meters (about 24 acres) of factory floor, and 2,600 machines of all types.

In the course of 15 years, while TREMEC had developed its manufacturing capacity and acceptable quality, it only possessed an incipient in-house design capacity and little awareness of world market trends.

In 1980 the world automotive market changed drastically due to the competition of Japanese cars and the quality of European imports, which affected the U.S. market, and consequently the Latin American market. Meanwhile automobile transmissions kept evolving, with many changing to front wheel drive, leaving our rear-wheel drive capacity idle. Pick-up gear boxes changed from 3 to 4 and even 5 speeds. In the 80s gradual changes to reduce the weight of transmissions, to make gear changing smoother, and to reduce transmission noise combined to raise the required quality standards. Towards the end of 1987, the automotive and parts industry was selected by the Government to initiate a process of change aimed at achieving international cost competitivity, with products technologically comparable to world standards. This has signified a virtual freeze on product prices, but not on the costs of raw materials, supplies, and wages which went on rising at inflationary rates.

The Most Important Changes

The life of the company can be divided into two clearly defined stages. Like many others in the motor industry, TREMEC started out 25 year ago in a country in the early stages of industrialization. Nineteen ninety started out with a new decree placing the industry in a framework of competition, without any kind of incentive, with additional taxes on assets, and in an open market that allows the unlimited import of automobile parts against the payment of a 10% import duty. The first stage lasted from 1965 to 1979, with 15 years of steady growth. The second stage, from 1980 to 1989, was one of technological changes and growth in both the domestic and export markets.

The First Stage

The first stage was characterized by the contrasts between the technical and cultural features of the foreign personnel as compared with the Mexicans, both at the executive level of the company and vis-à-vis customers and suppliers. The technical and cultural exposure of our personnel in an environment of constantly growing production, without a break, without an opportunity to refine programs and systems, and at times without the ability to detect errors, led us to establish production methods and systems that were effective short term, but created faults and omissions that were not detected until later. Besides, when one is successful, it is hard to believe one's luck could change. One goes on using the same formula that goes on growing when, in fact, it needs to be changed.

The Second Stage

Starting in 1980, changes took place in the areas of technology, culture, and labor relations, each requiring an appropriate response from the company.

The first of these was the change in internationally accepted quality standards. To deal with this, an Integral Quality Program was instituted. This included 'autocontrol' and customer service as the key features that enabled us to meet the new quality standards in automobiles. These were originally measured in the number of rectifications required per hundred units, and now this was modified to rectifications per thousand units—i.e., a tenfold quality improvement was required. This meant a profound change in philosophy with regard to quality, modifying former inspection practices and transferring these functions to the operator. The latter had to learn to prepare graphs, interpret results, and initiate corrective action, even to halt the production line when needed to correct some problem, which was a complete reversal of former practices.

Another program introduced was MRP (Manufacturing Resources Planning), which consists of establishing a computer-assisted planning process assuring that only what is needed at a given time is produced. This program has become an indispensable tool for satisfying the customers' requirement for JIT (Just in Time) deliveries to keep down their inventories. Without MRP the extra inventories would just have been transferred to our plant, saddling us with a heavy financial burden. This program also represented a great technological cultural shock, since it meant learning and/or understanding computers and exercising manufacturing discipline so that production would be started or stopped when the program said so, not when the production area wanted to. This program also modified the functioning of the service departments. It demanded more dedication and a greater spirit of service to give support to the production areas, changing also the former practices where production areas would request, and often beg for, the attention of the service departments. It goes without saying that this also produced structural changes in the organization, upgrading the level of the production areas and obliging them to change their personality profiles.

The management style used during the first 15 years of operation was frankly authoritarian and paternalistic. The company then looked for the type of person who had good technical knowledge, sound judgment, dynamism, and loyalty to his boss. When the first three were lacking, then loyalty to the boss predominated. As work was divided by areas, interrelationships between areas was very limited.

In 1982 the company embarked on a process of change to promote the forming of interdepartmental, interdisciplinary working groups at all levels. In this way it was sought to obtain the commitment and involvement of all members of the organization. The production lines were regrouped following the same concept by product type, to reduce inventories and to improve quality, even at the expense of under utilizing the equipment. But the market was slack, so it did not matter. At the management level, a product research and development program was set up to design and build our own transmissions. The help of several foreign nationals, as well as foreign and Mexican universities, was enrolled for the calculations involved in the design of transmissions, gears and components, using the latest computer technology. At the same time, a program of technological updating was undertaken in the fields of machinery, heat treatment, and metrology, partly financed by the sale of old equipment which no longer met the technical specifications of the new products. We also purchased modern computerized machines and measuring equipment, giving greater accuracy and higher productivity. This was complemented by an internal machine rebuilding shop, where servomechanisms, electronic controls, and computer systems were added. This brought the old equipment up to modern standards, albeit with limited life and flexibility, but at a very competitive cost.

The foregoing programs were supported by a general training plan at all levels of the organization. This was implemented simultaneously at all levels in several disciplines, covering technical aspects, philosophy and attitudes, so as to develop new skills and open up new perspectives for employees.

All these changes and programs were carried out successfully. This made it possible for the company to survive a cut back to one third its 1980 size: from 6,500 employees to 2,200; in active assets from 2,600 machine tools to 1,300; and in sales also to one half of 1989. Debts valued at $80 million were repaid and all the personnel laid off were liquidated according to Mexican law. The company made the adjustments to the new technologies and quality standards by a policy of continuous investment throughout this period.

The organizational climate prevailing during all this process was one of constant change, with ups and downs, in cultural and technological tensions among both Mexicans and foreigners, in a context of multiple dealings—i.e., as employees, suppliers, and customers. The turbulent environment, caused by 10 years of devaluations and inflation, added to the already considerable stresses provoked by the internal changes.

During the years 1988 and 1989 the external pressures caused by the removal of trade barriers and the Economic Solidarity Pact (a pact between Government, employers and unions, freezing prices and wages) rapidly forced us to be competitive in the domestic market with world prices and precipitated changes that had been foreseen for the decade of the 90s. We have faced the dilemma of changing our cultural values or maintaining them while trying to be competitive using the traditional Mexican industrial management style.

Within this organization is awareness that to achieve competitiveness is necessary, even indispensable, to have productivity, efficiency, discipline, on-time deliveries, as well as the practice of self control and dedication to one's work, carrying out one's functions with quality, and training to be better at the job. However, we are also aware that to achieve this, one has to be more objective, more demanding of oneself and others in the context of one's responsibility. At the supervisor, managerial, and executive levels corrective actions are required to stimulate people's capacity over and above personal and friendship preferences, and to be able to work with persons who are capable, though less close, giving loyalty to the job or the organization, rather than the person.

In the 90s the challenge facing TREMEC will be to become internationally competitive without depending on a depressed peso to dollar exchange rate or wages below world levels as a stimulus to exports. But we also need fewer people to watch and supervise that things get done and done well. Then the resources will be used better and the salaries will increase. ■

VII. Vacor de Mexico, S.A. de C.V.

Brief History

About fifty-five years ago a group of Mexican executives met in Mexico City and founded a company for the purpose of manufacturing a basic and attractive children's toy—marbles. Why exactly marbles? Well, because they are an economical toy, and since nobody was making them in Mexico, the founding partners launched this venture confident in their abilities and with vision for the future.

Among the founders were some members of the Vázquez-Cornejo family, who have continued to be active in the group since its beginnings, being later joined by their descendants.

But do not let us imagine that the success achieved by the company was a matter of chance. It was the result of a great investment of effort, dynamism, imagination, and energy that was necessary to make the business prosper, so that today it is the number one producer of marbles in the world.

The Most Important Changes, The Steps Followed in their Introduction, and the Results Achieved

Certainly the company has gone through some changes, both internal and external, the most important being:

The key change in the business was undoubtedly the decision taken some 15 years ago of entering the export market, having previously only supplied the national market. This decision forced the management to completely change the company philosophy, since on entering the international market they became aware of the very different way in which business was done as compared with the national market. They were also aware of the fierce competition, forcing them to make product quality the highest priority, and not merely an acceptable quality, but the best in the market. Second came customer service. Third, but hardly less important, was to provide these two at a reasonable price, so that the customer would never have to pay for our inefficiency.

As a result the owners had to open two more plants, one in Irapuato, Guanajuato, and the other in Guadalajara, Jalisco (the present VACOR DE MÉXICO). The beginnings were difficult and arduous, and lasted several years, during which the company went through a profound internal change. This affected the company philosophy and the attitude of top management toward this new outlook. The rewards were, however, considerable. It meant that this firm was converted into the world's number one producer of marbles, with all the benefits and advantages that this privileges brings, and all the responsibility it implies at all levels.

Another important change is the diversification in the use of our product. At the beginning and for several years afterwards the marbles were only produced for the toy market. With the opening of the export market other uses came to the fore: industrial, decorative, and for publicity. This obligated us to increase personnel training at all levels and to carry out research to adapt the technology to these changes. It should be pointed out that the technology is 100% the company's own. This has allowed the company to consolidate and to grow rapidly.

Other important changes include the closure of two plants (Mexico City and Irapuato, Guanajuato), the effects of rapid devaluations of the peso, high rates of inflation, and the price control pacts and exchange controls, all of which had to be attended to by the management and solved in the best way possible.

The Most Difficult Changes and the Obstacles Overcome

Certainly the most difficult obstacles to be overcome to effect change were lack of experience of Mexican industry in competing in the international market place. It proved necessary to change the mentality, not only of senior management, but of all personnel to achieve world class efficiency.

On the other hand the internal changes in the country also caused major problems, the most difficult being the imposition of foreign exchange controls that led to problems and confusion. These had to be overcome and in due course we made the necessary adaptations.

Advice and Recommendations for Companies Wishing to Make the Transition to Modern Management Practices

One of the most useful tools that undoubtedly was key to our success was our participation and attendance at major international events (shows, conferences) in our product area. From these we learned about new markets, observed the panorama of international competition, and found out about the latest production techniques.

On the other hand as mentioned earlier, the constant training and development of personnel at all levels was indispensable for a company wishing to maintain international standards. ■

Conclusions

These seven success stories describe varied experiences and circumstances that compelled Mexican companies to make changes in their management approach. Some of the common elements worthy of summary are:

The Vision of the Company

All these companies emphasized the important role of the breath of vision and leadership exercised by a small number of people. They set the underlying philosophy and the future direction that guided company development.

Participation

Critical to the success of these companies has been the total involvement of people at all levels, starting with senior management down to the lowest workers. This has meant that responsibility and authority were shifted to the lowest possible level, encouraging creativity and the unimpeded upward flow of ideas.

Communication

Great emphasis has been placed on developing an effective (and sometimes quite sophisticated) communications system, providing for the rapid two-way flow of information.

Training and Development

Every person in these companies has been given the opportunity to develop to full potential through carefully designed training programs.

Dedication to Total Quality

A common objective that pertains to these companies is Total Quality. This is reflected in the quality of work, product and service, and in terms of quality of life as a whole, including that of families.

In summary, these modernized Mexican companies have taken a totally new approach. Instead of passing down orders through the chain of command, senior management has recognized and harnessed the enormous potential of human resources. They recognize that the skillful development of people demands great effort, patience, and dedication. This can only be achieved when senior management believes in what is being done and is fully committed to the process. The benefits reaped by organizations that persevere speak for themselves in these stories.

Insights for U.S. Managers

U.S. managers working in Mexico need to heed the conclusions drawn above. In addition they should also take these points into account:

1) Cultural adaptation must be accepted as essential for success. Managers must be selected carefully based on their sensitivity and flexibility, as well as their sincere desire for the challenge of working in Mexico. After selection, these managers need to experience a period of cultural orientation and adaptation to be successful.
2) The way modern participative management works in Mexico is different from the U.S. Managers must recognize these differences and adjust the American style to the values and perceptions of Mexico.
3) A win/win philosophy is essential for long-term successful business opportunities in Mexico, as opposed to the traditional short-term win/lose philosophy.

Mexico and U.S. business has much to gain from each other. The transition period being experienced in both countries (and in Mexico more dramatically) can serve as the foundation for a long-term healthy and successful business relationship. The main ingredient for business success depends on the understanding of the differences in management style and philosophy in Mexico, and the ability to make the required adaptations.

Appendix

Exercise for Management Analysis

This exercise is provided to assist management in the process of self-analysis and evaluation. It is sufficiently flexible to be used by all levels of management, from the CEO down to the lowest management level.

Method of Application

1. Self-Analysis

The exercise consists of a detailed breakdown of the different factors and attitudes involved in two different approaches to management. On the left side is shown the traditional approach, and on the right side a composite of modern Mexican management. Between the two extremes are five columns labeled A to E, allowing participants to assess where they fit between these two styles. Parts I and II are for the CEO-owner only. Parts III to VII are for all management levels.

Few managers will find themselves (or their companies) at one extreme of the other on the scale. Most will be somewhere in between. Often participants will find that they may be quite traditional in some aspects but quite modern in others. This is normal during periods of transition.

Participants should also be aware of the common tendency to assess some aspects on the basis of what they feel is (or should be) company policy, rather than company practice and their personal way of doing things. In addition, some may be tempted to assess points according to what they believe the boss wants, instead of what really happens. What is important to bear in mind is that to derive maximum benefit from the exercise one should be as honest and objective as possible, thinking only about what really happens. This requires considerable soul searching in many areas, but without this sincere attempt at self-analysis the exercise becomes pointless.

2. Evaluation

This exercise may be used as a tool to evaluate an individual manager by (a) himself—auto-evaluation, (b) his superior, (c) his colleagues—lateral or peer group, or (d) his subordinates. This process, particularly in forms (c) and (d), must be planned carefully and the participants must be prepared well to be effective. Usually this requires the assistance of an outside facilitator.

3. Scoring

The steps followed in evaluating the results of each section are:

(1) Total the number of check marks (points) in each column to obtain a sub-total.

(2) Multiply the sub-total of each column by the appropriate factor—i.e., *A x 1, B x 2, C x 3, D x 4, E x 5*—and enter these in the boxes labeled Totals.

(3) Add up these totals to give the Total Score for the section.

(4) Match this total score to the Key to evaluate results for each section.

4. Analysis of Results

Once the exercise has been completed, an analysis can be made of specific strengths and weaknesses. This gives the CEO and the management team an initial picture of where the company stands at present. Based on this the company can take the first solid steps in the transition process. It must be underscored that the transition process begins with the CEO. It is, therefore, essential that he and all the members of the senior management team go through the analysis process. In addition, the exercise may be used throughout the transition process to evaluate progress and performance of individual managers.

Exercise for Self-Analysis

Part I Philosophy and Objectives
(For CEO and Senior Management only)

Traditional	A	B	C	D	E	Modern
a) Company philosophy is nonexistent or only implicit						Company philosophy is clearly stated in writing
b) Company philosophy incompletely understood and inconsistently practiced						Company philosophy clearly understood and consistently practiced
c) Overall objectives decided by CEO/owner						Overall objectives decided by senior management group
d) Overall objectives are general in nature						Overall objectives are specific in nature
e) Objectives are committed to memory						All objectives are stated in writing
f) Objectives are based on a 1 or 2 year time frame						Objectives are based on long-term (5 to 10 year) time frame
g) Objectives stress quick return on capital						Objectives stress long-term viability of business
Total a–g						
Times	1	2	3	4	5	
Sub-total Part1 (Carry over to Part 2)						----------------→

Exercise for Self-Analysis

Part II Planning
(For CEO and Senior Management only)

Traditional	A	B	C	D	E	Modern
a) Overall plans for achieving objectives decided by CEO						Overall plans for achieving objectives decided by Senior Management team (including CEO)
b) Priorities decided by CEO						Priorities decided by senior management
c) Time frame for overall plans decided by CEO						Time frame for overall plans decided by senior management team
d) Plans committed to memory						All plans put in writing
e) Time frames for plans viewed as desirable goals						Time frames for plans viewed as firm commitments
f) Overall plans not supported by detailed action plans						Overall plans supported by detailed action plans
Total a–f						
Times	1	2	3	4	5	
Sub-total Part II						
Carry-over Part I						
Total Parts I & II						

Total Score

Key: Parts I & II

13–20	Traditional Approach
21–35	First Signs of Change
36–51	Transition in Progress
52–61	Transition Advanced
62-65	Modern Approach

Exercise for Self-Analysis

Part III Organization

Traditional	A	B	C	D	E	Modern
a) CEO assigns responsibilities to managers orally						Sr. Mgt. Team & each Dept. Mgt. Team discuss plans & agree jointly on dept. responsibilities
b) Communication one way only						All communication is two ways
c) Almost all departmental problems and decisions referred to CEO for approval						Departmental manager has full authority for all decisions in his area
d) CEO assigns deadlines						Management teams decide deadlines based on overall plan
e) Action plans left to managers, not put in writing						Action plans made by management teams, put in writing
f) CEO decides priorities						Priorities decided by management teams based on overall plans
g) Time frames optimistic, no allowance made for possible problems						Time frames are realistic, with time cushions to allow for possible problems
h) Manager begins projects without detailed action plan						Manager begins projects based on detailed action plan
i) Manager prefers to do a difficult task himself, rather than risk mistakes by subordinates						Manager prefers to take the time and effort to teach his subordinates to do difficult jobs
Total a–i						
Times	1	2	3	4	5	
Totals Part III						

Total Score

Key: Parts III	
09–11	Traditional Approach
12–25	First Signs of Change
26–34	Transition in Progress
35–42	Transition Advanced
43–45	Modern Approach

Exercise for Self-Analysis

Part IV Delegation

Traditional	A	B	C	D	E	Modern
a) Manager assigns tasks to subordinate						Manager discusses activities with subordinate teams, who jointly agree on task assignment
b) One-way communication; subordinate expected to do as told						Two-way communication
c) Subordinate obedience emphasized						Subordinate participation and expression of views emphasized
d) Doubts and misunderstandings by subordinates not clarified						Strong emphasis on clarification of all doubts and misunderstandings
e) Subordinate fears to admit failure to understand some point						Subordinates readily admit any failure to understand and discuss it until clarified and agreed
f) Priorities not clearly defined						Priorities clearly defined based on action plan
g) Priorities routinely disrupted by unforeseen problems						Priorities rarely disrupted by unforeseen problems
h) Subordinates tend to interpret last task assigned as first priority						Priorities remain unchanged despite additional tasks
i) Subordinates routinely seek advice and approval for tasks to be performed						Subordinates feel confidence and proceed without soliciting advice or approval
j) The manager is expected to know all the answers to all questions						Manager is not expected to be an expert in every field, and he openly admits it
k) Lateral departmental working relationships are difficult and discouraged						Lateral interdepartmental working relationships are usual and encouraged
l) Manager spends most of working day in his office						Manager spends most of working day on plant floor
Total a–i						
Times	1	2	3	4	5	
Totals Part IV						

Total Score

Key: Part IV	
12–20	Traditional Approach
21–35	First Signs of Change
36–47	Transition in Progress
48–56	Transition Advanced
57–60	Modern Approach

Exercise for Self-Analysis

Part V Control and Follow-through

Traditional	A	B	C	D	E	Modern
a) Delegated work not followed up by superior						Superior continuously follows up on work with teams
b) Follow-up does not occur until problems arise						Follow-up is routine to prevent or anticipate problems
c) Concept of sense of urgency not understood						Sense of urgency present at all times
d) Manager feels he should not have to follow-up on subordinates' work						Following up on subordinates' work is important part of manager's job
e) Subordinate feels threatened when superior checks on his work						Subordinate is confident that superior wants to help when he checks
f) Manager does not feel fully accountable for the performance and behavior of his subordinates						Manager feels fully accountable for everyone and everything that happens in his department
g) Manager tends to blame subordinates when problems arise						Manager blames himself for insufficient training if problems arise
h) Errors and potential problems usually reported too late for remedial action						Errors and potential problems reported as soon as noticed to allow for remedial action
i) Subordinates tend to give only positive feedback						Feedback is open and realistic, whether positive or negative
j) Subordinates often pretend to understand instructions, even when they do not						Subordinates ask questions until they are certain they fully understand
k) Good intentions are an acceptable substitute for getting a job done on time						Good intentions are not an acceptable substitute for getting a job done on time
l) Subordinates often use their resourcefulness to "fix" defective parts even though quality may be inferior						Subordinates reject faulty items as soon as they are detected and investigate the causes, so as to maintain quality standards
Total a–l						
Times	1	2	3	4	5	
Totals Part V						

Total Score

Key: Part V	
12–20	Traditional Approach
21–35	First Signs of Change
36–47	Transition in Progress
48–56	Transition Advanced
57–60	Modern Approach

Exercise for Self-Analysis

Part VI Evaluation of Managers

Traditional	A	B	C	D	E	Modern
a) One way communication						Two-way communication
b) CEO judges the manager on the basis of his perception of the manager's overall performance						CEO and manager together assess performance based on results—fulfillment of agreed objectives
c) CEO assesses the manager's personal qualities on the basis of loyalty, dedication, and obedience						Manager is evaluated by CEO, colleagues, and subordinates on personal qualities—human relations, cooperation, initiative, training of subordinates
d) Purpose of evaluation is to let manager know where he stands with his superior						Purpose of evaluation is to provide an opportunity for the manager to discuss his strengths and weaknesses and plan his strategy for improvement
e) Promotion—First considerations are family connections and influences						Promotion—First considerations are ability and performance
Part VII Training & Development						
a) CEO and Senior Management see their training role one of giving orders and ensuring they are carried out						CEO and Senior Management see their role as one of passing on knowledge and developing managers
b) Training usually takes form of outside courses or some general or technical topic						Training involves daily coaching, team meetings, with outside courses where needed
c) Outside courses usually theoretical, knowledge difficult to apply in the workplace						Outside courses are specific and concrete, with knowledge directly applicable in the workplace
d) Evaluation of course consists of verbal report of manager's opinion to the CEO						Courses are evaluated on the basis of results of application of knowledge gained
e) Cost effectiveness of training is not measured						Cost effectiveness of all training is measured on the basis of strict criteria
Total a–e, Parts VI-VII						
Times	1	2	3	4	5	
Totals Part VI-VII						

Total Score

Carry to Next Page

Exercise for Self-Analysis

Part VII Training & Development (Continued)

Traditional	A	B	C	D	E	Modern
f) Managers see training as a recognition of their value, while also hoping to learn something interesting and useful						Managers see training as an opportunity for improving their performance and development for future promotion
g) CEO unwilling to adopt new techniques learned by managers if these threaten his traditional style						CEO is open to any new ideas learned by managers if they can improve quality and efficiency

Training of Workers: Manager Responsibilities

Traditional	A	B	C	D	E	Modern
h) New workers learn from experienced workers						New workers placed on formal program: classroom and special on-the-job training
i) Manager does not view himself as a teacher (trainer)						Manager views training as one of his most important jobs
j) Manager sees his role as a director of people rather than a developer of people						Manager sees his role more as a developer of people than a director of people
k) "Training"—i.e., giving orders, is a one-way process						Training and development is a two-way process of communication
l) Training is considered a drain on the budget with few tangible benefits						Training is considered an investment which will pay for itself many times over
Sub-Total f-l						
Times	**1**	**2**	**3**	**4**	**5**	
Sub-Totals Part VII						

Carry over score + **Total Sub-Score**

= **Total Score VI-VII**

Key: Parts VI & VII

17–26	Traditional Approach
27–49	First Signs of Change
50–64	Transition in Progress
65–79	Transition Advanced
80–85	Modern Approach

Bibliography

Alba Vega, Carlos, and Dirk Kruijt. "Los Empresarios y la Industria de Guadalajara." Guadalajara, 1988.

Arias Galicia, Fernando, (Coord.). "Administración de Recursos Humanos." Mexico: Ed. Trillas, 1980.

Beckhard, Richard. *Organizational Development: Strategies and Models*. Reading, MA: Addison-Wesley, 1969.

Bennis, Warren G.. *Changing Organizations: Essays on the Development and Evolution of Human Organizations*. New York: McGraw Hill, 1966.

Bloom, Allan. *The Closing of the American Mind*. New York: Simon and Schuster, 1988.

Camarena, Jorge, and Pablo Lasso. "Hacia un Estilo Proprio de Dirección de Empresas." Washington, D.C.: ITESO/BID, 1984.

Castaneda, Jorge G., and Robert A. Pastor. "Limites en la Amistad." México: Ed. Joaquin Moritiz/Planeta, 1989.

Craig, Robert L., and Lester R. Bittle. *Training and Development Handbook*. New York: MCGraw-Hill, 1967.

Crocker, Olga L., Syril Charney, and Johnny Sik Leung Chiu. "Quality Circles." Agincourt, Ontario, Canada: Methuen Publications, 1984.

De la Cerda,José,and Francisco Nuñez. "La Administración en Desarrollo: Problemas y Avances de la Administración en México." México: Xache-te-ITESO, 1990.

Dowling, Peter J., and Randall S. Schuler. *Human Resource Management*. Boston: PWS-KENT Publishing Company, 1990.

Drucker, Peter F.. *The Frontiers of Management*. New York: Harper and Row, 1986.

Drucker, Peter F.. *The Changing World of the Executive*. New York: Random House, 1985.

Fernandez Arena, José Antonio. "Seis Estilos de Administración." México: Ed. Diana, 1984.

Ferner, Jack D.. "Administración del Tiempo Como Recurso." México: Ed. LIMUSA, 1980.

Fordyce, Jack K., and Raymond Weil. *Managing With People: A Manager's Handbook of Organizational Development*. Reading, MA: Addison-Wesley, 1971.

Gibson, James L., John M. Ivanevich, and James H. Donnelly, Jr. *Organizations: Behavior, Structure, Processes*. 3rd Edition, Business Publications Inc., 1979.

Gonzalez Pineda, Francisco. "El Méxicano: La Psicologia de su Destructividad." México: Ed. Pax, 1975.

Greiner, Larry E. "Patterns of Organization Chamge." *Harvard Business Review*, May-June, 1967 (Harvard Library, Series V, No. 90).

Greiner, Larry E. "Evolution and Revolution as Organizations Change." *Harvard Business Review*, July-August, 1972 (Harvard Library, Series II, No. 25).

Harman, Willis W. *Global Mind Change*. Indianapolis: Knowledge Systems Inc., 1988.

Hernández Medina, Alberto, and Luis Narro Rodríguez (Coordinadores). "Cómo Somos los Mexicanos." México: Centro de Estudios Educativos, 1987.

Humble, John W. *How to Manage by Objectives*. New York: American Management Association, 1973.

Hecht, Maurice. *What Happens in Management, Principles and Practices*. New York: AMACOM (Division of American Management Association,), no date, ISBN 0-8144-5586-7.

Huse, Edgar F. *Organization Development and Change*. St. Paul: West Publishing Company, 1980.

Illich, Ivan. *Deschooling Society*. New York: Harper & Row, 1970.

IMEF (El Instituto Mexicano de Ejecutivos de Finanzas). "Perspectivas de la Economia Mexicana y Oportunidades de Inversión." México: IMEF, 1987.

Iturriaga, J. "La Estructura y Cultura de México." México: Fondo de Cultura Economica, 1951.

Kliksberg, Bernardo. "Administración, Subdesarrollo y Estrangulamiento Economico." Buenos Aires: Ed. Paidos, 1972.

Kast, Fremont, and James E. Rosenzweig. *Administration and Management*. New York: McGraw-Hill, 1985.

Kras, Eva. *Management in Two Cultures*. Yarmouth, Maine: Intercultural Press Inc., 1988.

Kras, Eva. "Los Gerentes Mexicanos: ¿Están en Condiciones de Competir? México: IMEF, Vol. XVI, No. 8, Agosto 1987.

Kras, Eva, and Arthur Whatley. "Using Organizational Development Technology in Mexico: Issues and Problems." Victoria, Australia: *International Journal of Management*, in press.

Kotter, John P., and Leonard A. Schlesinger. "Choosing Strategies for Change." *Harvard Business Review*,, 1979 (Harvard Library, Series XIIII, No. 247).

Lafaye, Jacques. "Quetzalcoatl et Guadalupe." Paris: Ed. Gallimord, 1974.

Lasso, Pablo, and José de la Cerda. "Gerentes y Empresarios: Un Estudio Reciente en Guadalajara," México: *Management Today* (en Español), vol. XIV, No. 3, Sept. 1987, pp. 26-41.

Lawrence, Paul R. "How to Treat Resistance to Change." *Harvard Business Review*, May-June, 1954 (Harvard Library, Series I, No. 12).

Lewin, Kurt. *Field Theory of Social Science*. New York: Harper and Row, 1951.

Likert, Rensis. *The Human Organization and Value*. New York: McGraw-Hill, 1967.

Michael, Stephen R., et al. *Techniques of Organization Change*. New York: McGraw-Hill, 1981.

Miller, Lawrence. *American Spirit*, New York: Warner Books, 1985.

Ortiz Tirado Kelly, Javier. "Bimbo, Historia de Una Empresa Mexicana." México: Grupo Industrial Bimbo S.A. de C.V., 1985.

Ouchi, William. *The M-Form Society*. Reading, MA: Addison-Wesley Publishing Company, 1984.

Ouchi, Willian. *Theory Z*. Reading, MA: Addison-Wesley Publishing Company, 1981.

Pastor, Robert A, and Jorge G. Castañeda. *Limits to Friendship*. New York: Alfred A. Knopf, Inc., 1988.

Paz, Octavio. "El Laberinto de la Soledad." México: Fondo de Cultura Económica, 1959.

Peters, Thomas, and Robert Waterman. *In Search of Excellence*. New York: Warner Books, 1984.

Pozo Pino, Jaime. "Productividad." Monterrey, México: Ed. Futuro Latinoamericano S.A., 1983.

Prawda, Juan. "Teoria y Praxis de la Planeación Educativa en México." México: Ed. Grijalbo, S.A., 1985.

Reddin, W.J. "Cómo Vencer La Resistencia al Cambia." México: INFOTEC, Alta Direc., Vol. 24, No. 140, (July-August, 1988).

Rehder, Robert R. *Latin-American Management Development and Performance*. Reading MA: Addison-Wesley Publishing Company, 1968.

Riding, Alan. *Distant Neighbors: A Portrait of the Mexicans*. New York: Alfred A. Knopf, Inc. 1984.

Sachs, Wolfgang. "On the Archaeology of the Development Idea." London: *The Ecologist*, Vol. 20, No. 2, March/April 1990.

Serralde, Alejandro. "El Estilo Mexicano de Dirigir." México: Management Today en Español, Janaury, 1987, pp. 5-20.

Servitje, Lorenzo. "La Revalorización de la Empresa Privada," México: Ed. LIMUSA, 1983.

Soria, Victor M. "Relaciones Humanos." México: Ed. LIMUSA, 1983.

Walton, Mary. "Cómo Administrar con el Método Deming." Bogota, Colombia: Ed. Norma S.A., 1988.

Index